W9-CNN-272

*For Melinda,
with love from
Barbara*

Private Correspondence

Esther Tusquets. Photo by Mario Muchnik.

Private Correspondence

Esther Tusquets

Translated and with an Introduction by

Barbara F. Ichiishi

Lewisburg
Bucknell University Press

©2008 by Rosemont Publishing & Printing Corp.

All rights reserved. Authorization to photocopy items for internal or personal use, or the internal or personal use of specific clients, is granted by the copyright owner, provided that a base fee of $10.00, plus eight cents per page, per copy is paid directly to the Copyright Clearance Center, 222 Rosewood Drive, Danvers, Massachusetts 01923. [978-0-8387-5686-7/08 $10.00 + 8¢ pp, pc.]

Associated University Presses
2010 Eastpark Boulevard
Cranbury, NJ 08512

The paper used in this publication meets the requirements of the American National Standard for Permanence of Paper for Printed Library Materials Z39.48–1984.

Library of Congress Cataloging-in-Publication Data

Tusquets, Esther.
  [Correspondencia privada. English]
  Private correspondence / Esther Tusquets : translated and with an introduction by Barbara F. Ichiishi.
     p. cm.
  Includes bibliographical references.
  ISBN 978-0-8387-5686-7 (alk. paper)
  1. Tusquets, Esther. 2. Authors, Spanish—20th century—Biography. I. Ichiishi. Barbara F. (Barbara Franklin), 1948- II. Title.

  PQ6670.U8Z46 2008
  863'.64—dc22
  [B]
                                        2007039064

PRINTED IN THE UNITED STATES OF AMERICA

Contents

Acknowledgments

I WOULD LIKE TO EXPRESS MY GRATITUDE TO A NUMBER OF PEOPLE WHO have contributed in various ways to the realization of this book. My heartfelt thanks go to Isabel Guerra McSpadden for her careful reading of the translation text and her invaluable comments and suggestions. I am also very grateful to an anonymous Bucknell referee for her or his thorough and insightful report on the manuscript. Sincere thanks to my fine copyeditor, Sally Morton, and to Judith García Quismondo, Marilyn Pugliese, Janet Fishman, Jeffrey Ankrom, and Bob and Connie Greenspan for their excellent ideas and advice concerning various aspects of the project. As always, eternal thanks to my husband, Tatsuro, for his steadfast guidance and support on this as on every project I have undertaken over the years.

On a special note, my deep gratitude goes to Adriana Méndez for her inspiring guidance of my work on Esther Tusquets during my doctoral studies at the University of Iowa and in the years since. Finally, I would like to express my appreciation to Esther Tusquets for her kind assistance with the translation project, and for the extraordinary beauty with which she has graced my life.

Introduction

BARBARA F. ICHIISHI

ALTHOUGH THE CATALAN ESTHER TUSQUETS' CAREER AS AN AUTHOR began relatively late, when she was in her early forties, her passion for literature and belief in the power of words to shape reality have informed her life since early childhood. Born into an upper-middle-class Catalonian family on August 30, 1936, in the opening weeks of the Spanish Civil War, she grew to adulthood during the early years of the repressive Franco regime. Her father, Magín Tusquets, was a gifted doctor who provided for his wife Guillermina Guillén and their children Esther and Oscar a comfortable way of life. Esther's parents were privileged members of Catalan society, but from an early age their daughter felt at odds with the superficial and exclusionary values of her social class, sympathizing instead with the plight of the marginalized, the oppressed, and the misunderstood. Unhappy both in the familial sphere, due to her alienation from a cold and domineering mother, and in the wider social climate, as a young girl Tusquets turned to literature (fairy tales and myths, then novels, short stories, and plays) with fervor to find in the rich world of the imagination a compensation for disappointing reality. After attending the prestigious Colegio Alemán for her secondary education, she went on to study philosophy and literature at the Universities of Barcelona and Madrid, specializing in history. Soon after her graduation in 1959 she made a lifelong commitment to the promotion and dissemination of literature. From 1960 until her retirement in 2000 she directed a small but distinguished Barcelona publishing house called Editorial Lumen, which under her leadership developed a solid reputation for contemporary Spanish literature, translations of foreign classics, and children's books.

In 1978, three years after the death of Francisco Franco, Tusquets came out with her first novel, *The Same Sea as Every Summer*, which

9

owing to the daring nature of its subject, a lesbian affair between a middle-aged woman and an adolescent girl, and the highly erotic imagery
and prose style, caused a sensation in newly awakened Spain. In the following years more books appeared in rapid succession, forming a trilogy of novels about the sea, then an expanded series of interrelated
works that are stunning for their polish and originality. To date Tusquets has produced five novels and two autobiographical works, three
collections of short stories, and two children's tales.[1] Her works have
been highly praised on both sides of the Atlantic; two of her books won
the "Premio Ciudad de Barcelona" (1979, 1997). Her books have a
wide readership in Spain, especially among women, and have thus far
been translated into eight foreign languages. She figures regularly on
the reading list of Spanish literature courses at universities throughout
the United States.

Tusquets is now recognized as one of the most innovative writers of
twentieth-century Spain.[2] Her narrative cycle is known for its deep exploration of female psychology and sexuality, an exploration that unfolds through the combined working of content and form (narrative
structure and style). Her constant focus is on love, or human communion: the meaning of love, and the impact of its presence or absence on
the individual and on society as a whole. She sees the interrelatedness
of various forms of love, from the primal bond linking mother and
child to adult heterosexual, homosexual, and bisexual modes of attach-
ment. In showing the beauty and importance of all forms of love, she
offers a uniquely feminine vision which is inscribed through narrative
structure and through her daring play with language itself. The cir-
cular, spiraling form of her novels, a continual going over the same
ground of concerns each time at a higher level of awareness, expresses
the search for understanding and union between her past and present
selves, for harmony between self and world. Through her fluid musical
style, her long winding sentences that follow the logic of feeling states,
her writing dissolves the barriers among different modes of sensuality
and illuminates the tie between the erotic and the emotional life. For
Tusquets writing, like love, is ultimately the attempt to overcome one's
basic solitude and bridge the gulf between self and other, thereby discovering in the experience of intimacy the wonder and meaning of life.

In Tusquets' narrative world the fictional and the autobiographical
dimensions are closely allied. One finds in her works a continual shaping and reshaping of a small number of basic elements: characters, sit-

uations, themes. And beneath the apparently changing constellation of fictional characters and plots, her books constantly spin the same underlying tale, inscribing an extended female odyssey toward enlightenment and growth. Each novel of what is now considered to be her tetralogy repeats the same basic emotional situation: a middle-aged woman, wife and mother, goes through an emotional crisis that shakes her world to the core, a crisis involving the failure of romantic love. This tragic loss impels her on a journey inward and backward in time to solve the mystery of the course her life has taken. The voyage becomes an unconscious pilgrimage in search of the lost mother and the satisfactory primal bonding she did not receive as a child and which she needs in order to live and thrive. From a psychoanalytic perspective, the series of novels are an attempt to "work through" the emotional issues of her life story, to find catharsis and healing in the act of writing itself, and to gradually foster a more mature, forward-looking view of life through the characters and stories she creates. In conjunction with this developmental story is a withering critique of the superficial materialist values of her social milieu of upper-middle-class Catalonia, which on a broader level appears to encompass the attitudes and norms of Western patriarchal society as a whole. She seeks to subvert the belief systems that have formed her female protagonists by showing what happens to people who grow up in a world without the life-affirming values of intimacy and love.[3]

In her narrative cycle Tusquets has spun a subtle and elusive imaginary web using as raw materials the events of her own life and the lives of those around her. Thus for ardent readers of her fictional works and for newcomers alike, the importance of her 2001 memoir *Private Correspondence* cannot be overstated. A beautiful work in its own right, it is also the only book of the series which the author has said is almost purely autobiographical in content,[4] and as such provides the missing "key" to a complete understanding of her literary *oeuvre*; it is no wonder that its arrival was heralded by Mirella Servodidio as "a cause for celebration."[5] Here at last Tusquets offers us the "true" story that forms the psychological framework of her narrative corpus. The book consists of four chapters, each constituting an imaginary letter to one of the most important people of her life, now dead or dying, in which she reviews and meditates on her relationship with each and the role he or she has played in her story. The first letter is directed to her mother, the compelling figure who came to life in her first novel.[6] Here we see at close range this overpowering woman, glamorous, arrogant, clever, whose boundless egoism and emotional shortcomings marked her daughter forever. The second letter is to her high school literature teacher, her first adolescent love, a charming Andalusian gentleman who awakened her to her femininity. The third is addressed to Eduardo, an iconoclastic young playwright whose drama she acted in and with whom she had an impassioned relationship during her university years, a liaison which allowed her to break out of the norms of her parents' inbred social world. And the fourth letter is to the idealistic social activist Esteban, father of her children and the culminating love of her life. Written in the characteristic Tusquetian style, this sentimental history has the lyrical flow of a private conversation in which one pours out one's deepest thoughts and feelings to the chosen interlocutor in a quest for understanding. Each of these vital attachments represents one stage of her existence and of her emotional/intellectual development, and each letter likewise vividly evokes the era in which her personal drama was played out: her post-Civil War childhood in an upper-middle-class Catalan home, her 1950s adolescent secondary studies at the Colegio Alemán, her college years at the University of Barcelona, and her early adult life in the sixties and seventies amid the left-wing intelligentsia of the city. Together they show the interplay of the personal and the social over the forty-year course of Francoist Spain, as viewed through the lens of a woman's inner world.

For avid readers of Tusquets' fiction, it is illuminating to be introduced to the central figures in her life story who were to evolve into the cast of characters in her fictional works. The characters who are only shadowy, mysterious presences in her novels and stories, as seen through her female protagonists' darkly tinted glasses, are fleshed out in her memoir, so we get a sense of who their models were and what made them tick. Underlying Tusquets' works is a perpetual oscillation or tug-of-war between past and present: a tension between the urge to move forward into a fresh new future and a continual turning backwards, an impossible yearning back to the source to rewrite her life story. At that source, representing one pole of her vital experience, is the primary relationship with her mother, the unrequited love story which left a gaping hole in the daughter's spirit that can never be completely filled. The quest for the lost mother is the point of departure and the subtext of her first novel, *The Same Sea as Every Summer*, which opens with midlife protagonist Elia's return to her now vacant childhood home in pursuit of the phantom from the past who has never ceased to inhabit her daughter's inner world. In contrast to the ghostly portrayal of the maternal figure in that novel, Tusquets' "Letter to my mother (goddess most divine)" in *Private Correspondence* showcases the mother in action at the height of her powers in the context of her elitist social world. A woman of privileged background and of many and diverse gifts, she holds sway over those around her through her personal magnetism and her freethinking unconventional ways, which are all the more striking during the early years of the repressive Franco regime. From driving a motor car to her own avant-garde fashion creations to her heterodox readings and deliberate flaunting of Catholic mores of the period, she is a force to be reckoned with and an object of the curiosity, admiration, or censure of her peers. And yet, constrained by familial and class beliefs about the proper role of woman, frustrated in her early wish to have a career as an architect or interior designer, she has no constructive outlet for her talents and wastes her abundant energies in a round of frivolous social activities. She vents her unhappiness on her vulnerable young daughter, who despite being of an entirely different cast she relentlessly tries to mold in her own image. Tusquets as a child is both seduced and terrified by the force of her mother's personality, and never knows the joy of being seen and accepted for who she really is. From the author's current perspective as a mature woman who is revisiting the world of her childhood, her letter becomes a scathing indictment of the mother's mode of interpersonal relations and way of life. In both fact and fiction, the mother serves as the fixed point of origin out of which all else necessarily unfolds, exerting a determining influence on the trajectory of her daughter's life.

At the other pole of the author's vital experience is her passionate relationship with Esteban, the supreme love of her life, the story of which is related in the memoir's final letter, "Letter to Esteban (at last the Flying Dutchman)." Esteban plays a crucial role throughout Tusquets' narrative cycle: in the first and third novels (*The Same Sea as Every Summer* and *Stranded*) as the protagonist Elia's lover/husband, the idealistic Jorge, and in the fourth novel (*Never to Return*) as Elena's film director husband Julio. The vicissitudes of Tusquets' real love relationship with Esteban, with its dramatic falling in and ultimate falling out of love, form the axis of each of her fictional love stories, where the catalyst of the tale is a crisis arising out of the real or perceived failure of romantic love. The nature and outcome of each of these relationships in turn chart the course of the spiritual odyssey of their creator. In the first book the idealistic foreigner Jorge appears during the protagonist's adolescence and represents an escape route, a way out of the stifling hold of her mother and the superficial lifestyle of her social class into a more genuine, purposeful existence. But her white knight thwarts all her accumulated hopes and dreams by taking his fate in his own hands, abruptly committing suicide without giving her a word of advance warning or leaving behind a heartening message of farewell. This unprecedented act, which she interprets as an abandonment and a betrayal, thrusts her back into her mother's sphere of influence, leading to her marriage to the eligible bachelor Julio and her perpetual enslavement to her parents' alien world. It is only years later through her love affair with the adolescent Clara that the now middle-aged Elia finds compensation and healing for the wounds inflicted in her early life, a beautiful albeit fleeting interlude in the void of her existence.

The Jorge character reappears in the third and final work of the original trilogy in a form that more closely reflects the author's own experience. In *Stranded* Jorge is the writer Elia's cherished husband, with whom she has shared years of a fulfilling relationship and who is father of her son Daniel. However, the story again begins with the heroine in a state of crisis, here brought on by Jorge's sudden pronouncement that he no longer loves her, and from this point on the book depicts the heroine's working-through of this devastating new reality, an attempt to understand what has happened and gain the strength to move on with her life. Inner growth is evinced not only over the course of the novel but over the course of the series as a whole, through the perspectivism of the third novel, written from the shifting viewpoint of four characters in turn, which relativizes and broadens Elia's limited experience and world view; in the more subtle and multifaceted understanding of Jorge (a delving into his possible feelings and motivations) which goes along with the protagonist's new recognition and acceptance of the part she may have played in the failure of their relationship; and in the inspiring outcome of the story: her courageous embrace of a new independent future, fueled by her writing and her maternal love for her son. Elia's breathtaking twenty-two-page final monologue, which offers inspiration to those who may have suffered a similar misfortune in their own lives, is also the express "article of faith" of the author her-

self, of a woman who had the strength not only to raise her two children alone but to knead the painful facts of her story into the stuff of
great art.

The forward movement that is manifest over the course of the trilogy takes a different form in her fourth novel, *Never to Return*, with the
recasting of the love story, this time between Elena and her renowned
movie director husband Julio. Elena's midlife crisis, brought on by her
husband's departure to New York to celebrate the premiere of his latest
film with a younger woman, leads to another introspective probing of
self and world, this time through the medium of Freudian psychoanalysis. The humorous ironic tone of her account serves to distance the
protagonist from her own experience (of psychoanalysis and of life) and
to deflate the grandiose notions she has held since childhood, such as
her belief in the mythos of romantic love and in prevailing psychological and sociological doctrines concerning the nature and role of
woman. The book is unique in Tusquets' *oeuvre* in that the love story
has a "happy" ending; but although Elena and Julio's love *does* survive,
it does so in a tarnished state, for Elena has come to see more realisti-
cally the limitations of her self-centered spouse. As a complex work
which reflects the ambiguities of the authorial point of view, in its final
pages the jury is still out as to the efficacy of psychoanalysis and the
heroine's future. But one can optimistically surmise that Elena's new-
found self-confidence and final decision to continue with the analysis
may open new avenues to self-development.

Akin to the maternal figure in *The Same Sea as Every Summer*, these
principal male characters are in general not physically present in the
author's fictional works, since the author's intent is to inscribe an inner
developmental journey which plays out after the fact and can only be
effectively realized in their absence. The vague silhouettes of Jorge and
Julio which we find in Tusquets' novels take on flesh and bones in her
factual account of the life story of Esteban and of their relationship. In
Private Correspondence Esteban appears as the social idealist whose path
is determined by a set of historical circumstances that are beyond his
control, by the advent of the Spanish Civil War and the ensuing global
conflict. His early allegiance to the Republican cause leads him to
abandon other interests and ambitions, to give up the desire for a college education in order to work as an underground agent for the Allies
during the Second World War, resulting in imprisonment followed by
a prolonged expatriation in Latin America with accompanying social

and cultural estrangement. He returns to Spain forty years old and penniless, having lost all of his substantial earnings as a business executive in Venezuela. Furthermore, during his early life in Spain having been deflowered at the age of fourteen by his mother's best friend, he develops into a notorious Don Juan known for his seductive charms and subsequent abandonment of a wide array of women, who notwithstanding proves capable of engaging in a deep and genuine love in his bond with Esther. The latter speculates in her autobiographical account that Esteban may well have been seeking in their love compensation for all the frustrations and disappointments he had endured over the course of his life. This in turn might have placed too much weight on the relationship, creating a strain for them both which might have contributed to its eventual demise. While many questions in his and their story remain unanswered, the male lover who remains in the shadows in Tusquets' novels, serving mainly to further the heroine's inner growth, here emerges into the light of day as a vibrant and poignant character in his own right.

The two other addressees of the author's sentimental letters are also reincarnated in her fictional work. In the case of the high school literature teacher there is just a fleeting reference in *Never to Return* to an exceptional teacher, more enlightened and stimulating than the norm in the repressed, lethargic Spain of the fifties. The anonymous literature teacher of her memoir is a traditional Andalusian gentleman of elegant dress and demeanor, with a deep love of literature and an enthusiasm for all things Spanish (from bullfighting to flamenco dancing) which is bound up with an unquestioning adherence to the values of religion, fatherland, and family. The author's girlhood infatuation for her charming teacher lights up and warms her adolescent years, until as a young adult she comes to realize the irreconcilable disparities in their core principles and approach to life.

The playwright Eduardo is a more complex and elusive individual whose psyche the author seeks to fathom in her "Letter to Eduardo (dialogues in the shadows)." In their university student relationship at the School of Theater Eduardo had poured out to her stories of his tempestuous childhood and adolescence, of the early death of his mother, his father's economic woes, and his traumatic relationship with an abusive stepmother. As a bisexual who has illicit relations both with boys and with older women, Eduardo veers between sexual promiscuity and an extreme form of religiosity, a fanatical devotion to the Catholic faith. Esther's desire to help the young man leads her into the dark recesses of the Catholic Church through an equivocal alliance with the handsome young priest Father Arturo, whose real motives in the case remain in the shadows. With her current hindsight as a mature older woman, she now sees that Eduardo was at bottom a fragile and insecure youth, seeking by every means possible the warmth and stability he had never known, who was endowed with a great creative gift that ultimately becomes a burden that is too heavy for him to bear. He finally flees from his artistic calling to look for security in the remote confines of a Bolivian monastery, then in a modest publishing job in Argentina, burying his past to start anew on the other side of the world.

Characters based on Eduardo and his relationship with Tusquets figure prominently in her 1981 story collection *Siete miradas en un mismo paisaje* (Seven views of the same landscape), which can be seen as a prequel to her novelistic series, offering episodes from the early life (childhood and adolescence) of the midlife protagonist of the tetralogy. Akin to the format of the novelistic cycle, the story collection relates remembered episodes in the life of a girl named Sara, whose age and superficial circumstances differ from one story to the next but who appears to maintain the same underlying viewpoint. The tales show rites of passage of a girl who is out of synch with the world around her, the exclusive materialistic world of her parents, of upper-middle-class Barcelona society. Two of the stories reveal the disjunctions she finds in a romantic relationship during her college years with a young man who hails from a world far removed from the sheltered, privileged ambience she has known. The story "En la ciudad sin mar" (In the city without the sea) is set in Madrid, where Sara (like the young Esther) is sent away to school for a year by her parents to separate her from her undesirable boyfriend Eduardo. Here, as in many of Tusquets' works, the male lover only appears in the frame of the tale, which focuses on a lesbian relationship between Sara and fellow student Roxana, resonating with the story of her first novel and a recurrent theme of her fiction.[7] The tale highlights differences between male and female values and perspectives, contrasting the egocentricity, ambition, and lack of understanding of Eduardo with the loving nurturance of Roxana, who initiates an affair with Sara that comforts and sustains the latter after her apparent breakup with her boyfriend. In both the story and the novel the protagonist finally betrays her female lover to return to an unsatisfactory relationship with a man.

The other tale, "He besado tu boca, Yokanaan" (I have kissed your mouth, Jokanaan), in essence parallels the Eduardo episode of *Private Correspondence*. It recounts the coming together of Sara and Ernesto, the gifted young student actress and the budding director/playwright, through their mutual love of theater; Sara's view of their romance as a longed-for escape from the oppressive environment she has known into an intoxicating world of art and social struggle; and the final rupture, borne of the disconnect between their so different backgrounds and perspectives, with the girl's disillusionment to find that for Ernesto, as for most men, love does not conquer all. In both factual and fictional versions the immediate obstacle to the couple's union is the girl's parents' rejection of a young man emanating from a world and with attitudes and mores they despise. In contrast to the true account in which the author's parents abruptly forbid her from acting in the student production of Eduardo's play, the story concludes with Sara's magnificent and seductive rendition of Wilde's *Salomé*. However, the final words make clear that the performance is to be the young woman's swan song as an actress and appear to mark the end of her belief in the redemptive power of art and love, as she capitulates to the estranging laws of her social world.

In Tusquets' subtle and constantly shifting permutations of her small cast of characters, Eduardo resurfaces in the fourth novel of the tetralogy, *Never to Return*, as protagonist Elena's close lifelong confidante and friend. In a sense this Eduardo is like the other side of the coin of the brilliant but emotionally unstable young dramatist in Tusquets' memoir who abandons it all for a religious vocation as a monk, then for a humble job in publishing. For her fictional Eduardo is the modern artist who, despite possessing a questionable degree of talent and never enjoying the fruits of success, is totally committed to his painting, willing to risk and sacrifice all for his artistic calling. Another loner and emotionally deprived individual, despite his failings both in his personal life and his work, Elena admires him for his single-minded purpose and devotion to the cause of art, qualities she has lacked in her own life as a would-be writer who has opted for the easier path of serving as assistant to her successful film director husband, an extension of the traditional roles of wife and mother. The bitter disappointment and condemnation found in the final paragraphs of Tusquets' letter to Eduardo in *Private Correspondence* for his weakness in turning away from his artistic destiny, are counterpoised to her fictional persona's expressed admiration for the failed painter Eduardo for "that absolute dedication, that total sacrifice on the altar of a single passion, painting, as an end in itself, not as a means to gain wealth, fame, women, praise, even a small piece of immortality," for the individual with the courage to embrace "the riskiest game of all, which could lead only to the finds of genius or to insignificance."[8]

In relating the life story of an individual and her personal ties, Tusquets' memoir also tells the story of an era, of the post-Civil War generation. Her tale is set against a backdrop of political upheaval and repression, of shattered lives, of unrealized private and public hopes and dreams. Different characters represent diverse social strata and points of view, ranging from the ultranationalist high school teacher for whom the Spanish language, culture, and religion are the endowments of a unique people with an exceptional historic destiny, to the freedom fighter Esteban, whose early adherence to the Republican cause impels him to spend his early adulthood crossing the Pyrenees repeatedly alone and on foot to relay messages to the Allies during World War II, in the ultimately frustrated hope that an Allied victory would signal the end of the Franco dictatorship, an endeavor which leads the young man to imprisonment, torture, and a prolonged exile in Latin America. We see the collaborative role played by the clergy in the early Franco regime, and governmental means of social indoctrination, such as the required courses for women of the Sección Femenina. We witness the repression and stagnation of the early Franco years, with their social polarities and tensions, their undercurrents of rebellion and unrest. From that point on we watch the gradual progression to the prosperous and liberated Spain of the post-Franco era, and see what it has wrought: a world of freedom, but for the idealistic artists and intellectuals of Tusquets' ilk, one that is not free from disillusionment. And all of this is offered us not in the dry form of a history text, with its facts and figures, but through the private stories of the memoirist and her recollections of those around her, the vivid personal details which bring to life the cultural history of twentieth-century Spain.

On another level, if Tusquets' narrative as a whole constantly blurs the line between fact and fiction, in her memoir she plays with the notion of the quasi-fictitious nature of autobiography itself. The book after all consists of four imaginary letters to addressees who were all dead or dying at the time of writing, so from whom there can of course be no response. Thus they are not real physical letters, but in essence a conversation with self which she has decided to share with the world. Indeed the playful title *Private Correspondence* titillates the reader with the prospect of savoring spicy personal confessions while pointing to the fact that these "private letters" are actually destined for a very public audience. The one-way epistolary form captures well the tensions, strengths, and limitations of the autobiographical genre, while it goes beyond this to distill Tusquets' view of the fundamental human condition. According to Nancy Miller, "The power of life writing in its various forms depends on a tension between life and text that is never fully resolved."[9] Autobiographies are generally written years after the events they relate, so the writer is of necessity distanced from the experiences described in time and (perhaps) in space. The human memory is unreliable, setting in relief certain aspects of events while erasing or distorting others. In writing her own memoir, Miller speaks of feeling "a certain melancholy—that sense of perpetual belatedness which is perhaps the definition of autobiography . . . However close you get—more documents, more photographs, more stories—there's always a gap separating you from what you want to know."[10] And indeed the ultimate threshold is set by the boundaries of one's own subjectivity, the limits imposed by one's particular body, mind, and spirit; as we are all aware, the same event may be experienced and remembered quite differently by different individuals, or by the same individual over time. The epistolary form of Tusquets' memoir is central to her world view because for this author, as for many women, people are by definition relational beings, for whom true fulfillment and a sense of wholeness are to be found in the context of meaningful ties with others. Yet these lonely letters, like her narrative works as a whole, continually point to the difficulty, if not impossibility, of transcending one's subjectivity to arrive at the "truth" of a common experience borne of genuine understanding and communion with a fellow soul.

Tusquets' unanswered letters, then, record the gulf between self and other, between past and present, between ignorance and knowledge, between writing and experience. In a life story the axis of which is human relationships, her unsent and unanswered missives attest to the lack of mutuality in bonds with other people. The letters reveal a series of failed or aborted relationships, of misunderstandings or disjunctions between people. In each case she is denied the occasion for the final meeting and coming to terms with the other in real life, whether this be due to the intransigence of a maternal figure who only grows harder and more impervious to her daughter's needs with old age, or to the obstacles imposed by time, distance, sudden illness and death. So for her the mystery is never fully resolved; she is left to ponder the course of each relationship and its meaning in an imaginary encounter with the other. Hence the letters are full of queries, hypotheses, blanks, meditations, and nostalgia, taking shape as a monologue in which she is trying to play both parts, to get inside the other's head and find the answers he/she never provided, in order to bridge the gap and finally bring the two together. Underlying her narrative is also a tension between the desire to know and the urge *not* to know the "truth," for another's version of the same events may be too painful or estranging for her to bear. In the case of the Eduardo story, for instance, once she is denied the longed-for reunion with him in Barcelona owing to Eduardo's sudden illness and death, when his close friend (and perhaps lover) from Argentina arranges to visit her in her home some months later to attempt to piece together the enigmatic life story of their mutual friend, she receives him so drugged on narcotics and alcohol that there is no possibility of meaningful communication. This may well suggest a conscious or unconscious effort to avoid realities that are too painful or banal to be endured, that are not attuned to her own deep desires and needs.

Yet this in turn leads to the positive side of the inevitable distance between life writing and experience. For it is the autobiographer's very lack of knowledge, her ignorance or uncertainty, that gives her the freedom to tell her stories in her own way, to construct a narrative which bestows meaning on her private experience. In positing an addressee, the memoir becomes a testimonial by means of which the writer's version of the past gets to be heard. In Tusquets' case the addressee finally goes beyond the designated letter recipient to become the anonymous reader. In committing her story to paper, the memoirist knows the joy of returning to past events and shaping the often baffling and chaotic raw materials into a work of beauty and meaning that in turn resonates with others' lives and inner experience. Writing autobiography is a highly personal creative act which in its appeal to an audience, in Miller's words, "mitigates loneliness and removes the partitions that appear to wall off the self from empathy or compassion."[11] As an author Tusquets is motivated by the longing to overcome isolation and estrangement, to find or create understanding and union with the other, on paper if not in real life. This overwhelming need, which is the impetus behind her autobiographical account, is also the driving force behind her body of work as a whole.

The book concludes with a moving epilogue, the twilight words of an individual for whom the past, through memory and desire, always informs and overshadows the present. In her final reflections the author conjoins the plane of the personal with the universal. Having written her sentimental history from a vantage point near the "end" of her time, from this perspective Tusquets views the loss of love in one's life as a foreshadow of death, the final closure. She declares that the termination of her relationship with Esteban was a watershed event, after which something fundamental changed. Since that occurrence she has been filled with a sense of transience and futility; as she explains it, where up to then she had been living "stories," from that time on she has only experienced "things," marking the end of her emotional life. And yet, as Luis García Jambrina wisely observes, it is from the very moment when her life story apparently draws to a close that the inverse process begins: the conversion of her life into literature.[12] Her narrative cycle becomes a Proustian quest to recover her lost paradises in a form that will transcend the passage of time. Thus in revealing to us the "true" story, her late autobiographical work opens the door to her fictional universe, in this way closing the circle of life and art.

NOTES

1. Tusquets' novelistic production to date is as follows: *El mismo mar de todos los veranos* (Barcelona: Editorial Lumen, 1978); translated by Margaret E. W. Jones as *The Same Sea as Every Summer* (Lincoln: University of Nebraska Press, 1990); *El amor es un juego solitario* (Lumen, 1979); translated by Bruce Penman as *Love Is a Solitary Game* (New York: Riverrun Press, 1985); *Varada tras el último naufragio* (Lumen, 1980); translated by Susan E. Clark as *Stranded* (Elmwood Park, IL: Dalkey Archive Press, 1991); *Para no volver* (Lumen, 1985); translated by Barbara F. Ichiishi as *Never to Return* (University of Nebraska Press, 1999); and *Con la miel en los labios* (Barcelona: Editorial Anagrama, 1997). Her autobiographical works are *Correspondencia privada* (Anagrama, 2001); and *Confesiones de una editora poco mentirosa* (Barcelona: Rquer Editorial, 2005). Her story collections include *Siete miradas en un mismo paisaje* (Lumen, 1981); "*La niña lunática*" *y otros cuentos* (Lumen, 1997); and "*Orquesta de verano*" *y otros cuentos* (Barcelona: Plaza y Janés Editores, 2002). Her children's tales are *La conejita Marcela* (Lumen, 1980); and *La reina de los gatos* (Lumen, 1993).

2. For example, in his article on Spain in *The Bloomsbury Guide to Women's Literature*, Stephen M. Hart speaks of the "unprecedented boom in women's writing" that arose during the post-Franco era of the 1980s and beyond. Declaring that this fertile

period centered on the novel, he goes on to say, "Although it is perhaps invidious to put writers in order of rank, the single most important New Wave novelist is Esther Tusquets, who is best known for her trilogy of novels: *El mismo mar de todos los veranos* (*The Same Sea as Every Summer*); *El amor es un juego solitario* (*Love Is a Solitary Game*); and *Varada tras el último naufragio* (*Beached After the Last Shipwreck*) [*sic*], which shocked the reading public with their frank treatment of female and lesbian sexuality" (New York: Prentice Hall, 1992), 79.

3. Barbara F. Ichiishi, *The Apple of Earthly Love: Female Development in Esther Tusquets' Fiction* (New York: Peter Lang, 1994), 13–22.

4. Mercedes Mazquiarán de Rodríguez, "Entrevista con Esther Tusquets," *Letras Peninsulares* 13, no. 2 (Fall 2000): 615. *Correspondencia privada* is Tusquets' only personal memoir to date. In 2005 she came out with a professional memoir, *Confesiones de una editora poco mentirosa*, which recounts her most noteworthy experiences as a publisher.

5. Mirella d'Ambrosio Servodidio, "Esther Tusquets, *Correspondencia privada*," *Revista Hispánica Moderna* 60, no. 1 (June 2002): 224.

6. The letter to her mother in *Correspondencia privada* is essentially a reprint of the story "Carta a la madre" that was written for the collection: Laura Freixas, ed., *Madres e hijas* (Anagrama, 1996), 75–93.

7. There is one other character who appears repeatedly in shifting forms in Tusquets' narrative, the young lesbian woman who has a love affair with the older female protagonist. In the three books of the original trilogy she appears as the sensitive, emotionally deprived adolescent Clara; in her story collection *Siete miradas en un mismo paisaje* she is Roxana, a fellow student living in Sara's dormitory in Madrid; and in her late novel *Con la miel en los labios* she is the seductive but emotionally unstable undergraduate Andrea. In contrast to her other vital attachments, the author has never directly referred to the relationship that served as the model for these fictional representations. However, there is abundant evidence to suggest that they are based on her intense relationship with her younger friend and fellow writer Ana María Moix. In Moix's 1978 interview of the author upon publication of the latter's first novel ("Esther Tusquets: Madame Lumen para los amigos," *El viejo topo* 24 [September 1978]: 64–67), the two women playfully recreate and allude to the liaison which was the source of the novel's plot. Tusquets in turn serves as the model for major characters in Moix's fictional works, the most obvious of whom is perhaps Eva, the protagonist Julia's older teacher of whom she is enamored in Moix's first novel, *Julia* (a book which the author dedicated to Esther Tusquets). This would appear to be the still missing piece in the narrative of Tusquets' life.

8. *ever to Return*, 105.

9. Nancy K. Miller, *But Enough About Me: Why We Read Other People's Lives* (New York: Columbia University Press, 2002), xiv.

10. Miller, 133–35.

11. Miller, 115.

12. Luis García Jambrina, "Cuatro cartas abiertas," *ABC Cultural*, June 2, 2001, 11.

Private
Correspondence

Letter to my mother
(goddess most divine . . .)

LAST NIGHT I DREAMED AGAIN THAT I WAS IN YOUR OLD HOME (THE ONE you both abandoned long ago, replacing the center of the city with an absurd residential quarter to which the bourgeoisie was migrating almost en masse, that priggish, rootless bourgeoisie we were a part of, soon after which my brother and I left home at almost the same time to get married—impelled, you said, by the lack of light, but also no doubt by that never-ending desire for change, perhaps as intense as my desire to have so many things remain the same—and that now—I discovered on one of my melancholy walks through the scenery of my past—is used as a retirement home), although it would be more appropriate to say just your home, because if in the first dwelling that you shared and where the two of us were born my father had to a certain extent imposed his own aesthetic sense and his ideas of comfort—it's true that in the photos of your wedding and honeymoon, only in those, you have a lost, bewildered look—in the new dwelling you chose everything starting with the apartment, which I remember as magnificent and which I dream about at night more and more often, maybe because the years spent there were the most intense period of my life, but which my brother recalls as tawdry and which years later would suddenly seem to you too dark. Around that time Papa had abandoned without resistance any semblance of power, or even of opinion, in the domestic sphere, including the children, to place it entirely in your hands. He did this in part, I now believe, out of a certain laziness, because he was overburdened with work; in part because it was customary in our social group (the husband ceded to the wife, and the wife to a greater or lesser degree delegated to the servants, the care and upbringing of the children), but also because it had come to be accepted knowledge that you did everything—or at least everything that interested you and that you em-

27

barked upon—better than anyone, and the suspicion had been surreptitiously planted that you were superior to the common run of humanity. (Later on, over the course of a life that has long since exceeded half a century, I have been in touch with some politicians, some business executives, a throng of writers, painters, architects, artists in general, who played more or less successfully at being gods, but those who did not know you in your prime do not have the slightest idea of what constitutes the irrevocable calling to divinity.) And it was not just that my brother and I, like so many other children, believed that we had in you the best of mothers (as for the idea that we might have had the best of fathers, it never occurred to us because you were there to prevent it, although to my amazement my brother dedicated to Papa his first book),* but that the small world that surrounded us took as accepted dogma, and my father was the first to proclaim it (you could not have been so divine, you know, without such a dedicated and devout high priest), your ineffable sublimity.

You were the tallest, the blondest, the one with the brightest eyes (I was blond at birth and appear blond in the photographs of my early infancy, but my hair soon degenerated to chestnut color, I had dull brown eyes, and despite belonging to a later generation and being nourished according to the strictest rules of the best of German child care manuals, which almost morally obliged me to, I never reached your height: I always fell short by four blasted centimeters). You were so tall, and so blond, and had such white and delicate and fine skin, and so blue were your eyes and gaze (a flashing, terrible gaze that, like the Gorgon's,* could leave us frozen in place, and you knew and relished this, you loved hurling your thunderbolts, like the first lady of Olympus or Valhalla),* that you were often taken for a foreigner (the fact of looking like a foreigner, from northern Europe of course, was valued highly in our family circle, and we strutted like peacocks when someone in London or Paris or Geneva thought we were natives of the country and asked us for directions or the time).

You were also the most intelligent (do you remember the time, when we were already grown up, when Papa ingenuously wondered out loud where on earth my brother and I had gotten our intelligence from, and you looked at him dumbstruck, unable to grasp such stupidity, and the two of us burst out laughing?). I have to admit that you never denied my being intelligent—and it did not even occur to you, something I am very grateful for, that as aunts and girlfriends warned, intelligence in women could be a defect to hide, a disadvantage, just as you never promoted the idea, and in those days this was rare, that marriage was the only destiny for women—but you set up and continue to make a subtle distinction: I may be intelligent, but I am not at all smart, since there is a disturbing imbalance in my mind, owing to which, despite being well endowed for study, for abstract knowledge in general, I am almost mentally deficient in my dealings with other people (so absurdly prone to believe whatever they tell me, especially to believe that they like me if they say they like me!) and in my approach to reality and daily life. You were also (although in your later years—before illness and old age made off with all, laid waste to all—and motivated no doubt by the desire to entertain, to surprise, to continue to be at the center of any gathering when it was inevitable that you would stop being there, you got accustomed to repeating the same stories, which were no longer savory or amusing, and began speaking in too loud a voice, as though you feared that no one would listen to you) the cleverest, the wittiest, the most scintillating; the fact that your biting wit often gave rise to the most cruel and heartless sarcastic remarks did not seem to bother anyone, except the person who on that specific occasion was their target, always surrounded as you were by a loyal circle of unconditional admirers, disposed to laugh at your wisecracks and ignore your excesses, all men, because—and this is not the least of your shortcomings—you have never been able to establish, no doubt because it did not interest you—you only feel comfortable with men, with them you feel among your equals, without this lessening your capacity for seduction—an important bond of affection with another woman, starting with your mother—in your growing ravings and nostalgia of recent years, in which old age confronts you with a world of shades and phantoms, there never appears the figure of your mother, whereas that of your father is a constant presence—and ending with your granddaughter.

I have almost no memories of the Civil War* (a kitten that must have fallen into the washtub and that we managed to save, a cut on my thumb from which I still have the scar, which I got helping to peel potatoes in the kitchen, a marching soldier who gave me a little flag) and none in which you appear, but there are two anecdotes that you have repeated to friends and strangers ad nauseam, and which for that very reason assume symbolic significance. The first story: one day you are taking a walk with me on the street, me in the baby carriage and both of us dressed with extreme simplicity, but a group of working women, according to you from the FAI,* starts harassing us and chases us off with the threatening cry, "There are still Fascists!" The second anecdote: in my maternal grandmother's home, where we took refuge fleeing the bombardments of the center of the city, there is almost nothing to eat, you are all suffering from terrible hunger and everyone devours whatever they can find—omelet substitutes, weeds they usually leave for the rabbits, flour porridge, chickpeas full of worms—but not my mother: you would rather die of hunger than down such rubbish; and you are so thin that you are reaching the point of invisibility, when they manage to find for you a real egg, laid by one of the few surviving chickens, and they serve it to you at the table (they are on the brink of starvation, Papa in hiding as a deserter from the Republican army and the rest women, but there was always a faithful servant at home who did the housework and waited at table, and my grandmother did not go out on the street a single day without wearing her gold medallions around her neck), but to general dismay, you are not capable of swallowing a bite and leave the egg on the plate. The moral: much as one may disguise oneself as a beggar-woman and live in wretched conditions, a genuine princess—one need only think of the princess and the pea,* although you, always wary and suspicious, changed the ending of the story when you told it to me so in your version it was a question of a cunning girl and not an authentic princess at all—always remains a princess!

Although I do not retain memories of you from the war years (I was born in '36), the postwar years—during which I abruptly and without understanding why went from being by your side every hour of the day and night to seeing the two of you very seldom, because Papa was working like a maniac, determined to gain the means, after the disaster of the armed conflict, to provide for the whole family, but first and foremost for you, a high standard of living which he considered (mistakenly, I think) to be indispensable for our happiness; and you, fed up with three years of confinement that had been almost like a prolongation of your earlier life as a single woman, were never home—are full of you. You drove the car, everyone said, and we were then in the early forties, as well as or better than any man; you swam an impeccable competition-level crawl, which I do not know where you had learned, because you seemed to know everything without having taken lessons in anything, dressed in a black knit bathing suit that clung like a glove to your skin, with no skirt or the least adornment, which no other woman on the beach—we are still in the prudish, terrible forties, when the law, obviously respected by almost no one, at least not in Catalonia,* made it obligatory to wear a bathrobe when you were not in the water and take it off at the water's edge at the very moment of bathing—would have dared to wear, even if they had had a body like yours. And in the finishing school you had attended for a few years, not very many, of course you had not learned to sew a hem or mend a tear, although you loved and you still love to grab some scissors and crazily cut and take things apart—you also loved to light huge fires in the fireplace that threatened to burn the house down, or hose down the garden so much that we practically had to cross it by boat, oh your excesses— and for years you were capable, by fits and starts, until your hands and your eyes gave out, of knitting fantastic garments of your own design, so that, when you felt like it and quick as you were in everything, in a few days there was a heap of stupendous sweaters and vests and scarves that we did not know what to do with. Nor had you learned—neither in high school nor in your parents' home, where your mother probably did not cook but taught and supervised the cooks, passing on to the new ones the customs and tastes of the household—to fry a steak or boil some vegetables. Many years later you would remark to me about a maid who was substituting for our sick cook for a few days: "I asked her to make me an omelet and it came out pretty badly, but of course, making an omelet must be very difficult . . ." Your culinary skills were limited to two delicacies; one playful and transgressive: to cook in the double boiler a large can of condensed milk and then down the whole thing—you, my brother and I—by spoonfuls or on a piece of toast; the other, almost magical: rice boiled for twenty minutes by the clock— you being a lover of clocks as objects and fanatic about punctuality (a fanaticism you shared for once with our father, because at home it was not that one was blamed for arriving late, it was worse, it was simply that one could not understand how such an absurdity could have occurred), even now when, hanging on the walls or laid out on the furniture, all your clocks have stopped or tell the wrong time—with no other seasoning than a pinch of salt, a stream of oil and a few cloves of garlic, thrown into the boiling water five minutes before the rice, capable of curing all ills of body and soul, and I wonder if my brother, now such a gourmet, has also confronted the problems of life taking refuge behind enormous plates of boiled rice.

ne thing for sure is that you left high school, or finishing in any case, your parents' home, knowing good French. You our two sisters read Zola, Balzac, and Voltaire* in the original, it had to be unusual that three little bourgeoises of the period were eading novels by authors who were on the index of books prohibited by the Church. My Lord, what would the members of Papa's grand, pretentious and ultraconservative family have thought and said if they had found out! Especially my grandmother and my prelate uncle who, when he came to your new home—the one I dream about so often—to bless it—during the postwar period and I do not know for how long after that, well-to-do people had their houses blessed before going to live in them—looked around feverishly but in vain for a painting or an image of the Sacred Heart—in the forties, and I do not know until when, respectable people had an image of the Sacred Heart presiding over hearth and home—until you finally took pity on him and glibly led him to an engraving of a head of Christ painted by Leonardo.* Although they certainly already sensed that you were not for them the ideal spouse—they were not even remotely as pleased with the marriage as your family was—and that you were not going to follow the rules of *The Perfect Wife** which they had given you, they could not suspect that by the time he married you, neither did my father believe in God (in fact he practiced a radical atheism that was quite far removed from your own agnosticism, an agnosticism that allowed you then and has allowed you even more in your old age to fantasize about the presence of the dead, a fantasy which for Papa was unimaginable), or that your own father—my maternal grandfather whom I regret not having met—not only was a Voltairean and a freethinker and contributed to unorthodox magazines, but was probably a member of a Masonic lodge.

So you left your parents' home knowing good French and acceptable English. And later, from scattered fragments you picked up during my classes with Herta—one of the good fairies of my childhood, perhaps the best, who filled in part the holes left by your absence—you would come to understand a little German.

When—for reasons I do not entirely understand, despite having spent a good part of my childhood and adolescence examining them and then having questioned you (to ask Papa was unimaginable)—at a very young age you agreed to marry a man you did not love, you did oil and watercolor painting, were adept at leather and metal embossing,

made hooked rugs (recently my brother showed us in a magazine com-
memorating graphic design of the twenties the rug that you copied
from some publication of the period and that for years lay beneath the
dining-room table), you decorated glass objects beautifully, you had
read more books than anyone I knew (at home there was always a real
library, that expanded day by day, made up of books that had been read,
not of encyclopedias and the complete works printed on India paper
and bound in leather that I almost always found in the homes of your
friends, usually in the husband's study) and without doubt had at your
disposal more stories to tell; and you did this better than any woman,
including your own sisters, since Scheherazade,* and in your case it
would not have taken a thousand and one nights to get the most misog-
ynous of sultans to spare your life and turn you into his queen. It is true
that you did not perform some of the roles that are generally assigned
to mothers, and that I desperately needed, but you filled our childhood
to the brim with condensed milk heated in the double boiler and with a
whole magical world of marvelous stories—taken for the most part
from fairy tales and classical mythology—that would shape our image
of the world.

It has been hard for me to halfway understand, or halfway forgive
(you consider that there is nothing in your life to be forgiven, and it is
possible that in this particular case you are right) the fact that when you
were not yet twenty years old and were being courted simultaneously
by several suitors (Papa, who knew few fairy tales—in his home they
must have only heard pious tales and the lives of saints—but who was
absolutely determined to transform you into a myth—he never questioned in our presence any decision that concerned us, he never gave us
permission to do anything without first referring us to you, thus turning you into mediator of all graces—gave us an explanation of your en-
gagement that made me think of the third brother,* the most foolish or
the most innocent, who ends up winning, to the general amazement,
the hand of the daughter of the king, or of Siegfried* of the Germanic
legends, which I knew from the Araluce Classics, who snatches the
Valkyrie* from her bed in flames), you condescended, fed up as you
were with the strict discipline of your father's home (you and your sisters were reading Voltaire, but the girls were not allowed, and this double standard was very common among liberals of the era, to take a step
outside the house without surveillance) and great as might have been
your naïveté about what married life involved (your father, such a

and bon viveur, whom you blamed for this senseless mar-
~~s perhaps of the stupid opinion, as was mine, that love comes
rd or that female sexuality is merely a copy of the male norm,
thing not even to be taken into account), so you condescended,
n, to get engaged to my father, who might have been an excellent
person and a good catch, who with another woman might have been a
magnificent husband, who might have charmed, as in fact occurred,
your entire family (everyone except you) and who without doubt loved
you deeply and passionately and would continue loving you like that—
and that was the most deplorable thing about your life together—until
his death, but whom you did not love. Were you aware in the past, or
have you been since, that on this point you did not leave my brother
and me, and from a very early age, the least shadow of a doubt, the least
glimmer of hope, because although you almost never argued in our
presence, much less raised your voices, or undermined each other's authority with respect to our upbringing—following to the letter, I suppose, the rules of the best German child rearing book, the most up-to-
date, today we would say the most politically correct, just as you had
followed with manic precision, perfectionist as you were in everything,
the rules governing our hygiene and nourishment—you always made it
abundantly clear—and why?—especially by your attitude, but also
openly by your words, especially in conversations with your sisters, two
other unhappily married women and I wonder if for similar reasons,
that you had never loved my father—I do not mean, of course, that you
did not feel a certain affection for him, but that you certainly did not
love him as a woman can love a man—at any time in the past, nor—he
was deluded if he had nourished such a hope—was there the remotest
chance of your loving him in the future? Are you aware that throughout my entire life I have seen you systematically degrade everything
about my father, whatever he did, whatever related to him—you as set
on scorning him as he on mythifying you—and that you have carried it
out with growing vehemence as the passing years have made you
harder, more frustrated, more bitter? Did you never notice—half witch
that you were who missed almost nothing, and pointed it out to us,
guessing correctly what we were doing, thinking, feeling—that my
brother and I blushed and drooled when we saw other married couples
your age spontaneously embrace, put their arms around each other's
shoulders or waists, kiss on the lips? Did you really think, Mama, that
my brother and I would ever be grateful for the fact that you did not

abandon him, that for our sake (now in my old age, far from the romanticism of youth, I realize that maybe you were afraid that abandoning him would mean abandoning us and that you never would have
been willing to leave us behind) you did not abandon him? Do you
think that beside this implacable lack of love it was of the slightest importance to us whether you had a hundred or one or no lovers, or
whether you lived out your affairs in plain sight or with scrupulous discretion?

But if it has been difficult for me to understand all this (to halfway
understand you, because Papa died an unfathomable secret to me, and
while I know for a fact that he loved you, I do not have too clear an idea
how he lived your story), it has also not been easy for me to understand
why—it could not just have been laziness, although a long life of inac-
tivity eventually led to your being extremely lazy—after your marriage
and my birth and the end of the war, you gave up all your activities, except reading. At home there were pieces of your handiwork: a good
copy of *The Anatomy Lesson*,* which hung behind the desk in Papa's
medical study, a small, exquisitely embossed metal chest where you
usually kept the bills, a set of parfait glasses decorated with geometrical
designs, the dining-room rug that you must have copied from a magazine around the time of Bauhaus,* but all these were already there
when I was born. And neither did you drop some activities to take up
others, because your work as a housewife (aside from replacing the furniture, changing overnight the layout of the rooms, installing doors
where there weren't any and tearing down walls) was always limited to
some days going over the grocery expenditures with the cook (the suc-
cessive cooks, who to a greater or lesser degree must have taken you for
a ride, because you have never had the slightest idea—or me either,
why deny it—of what a kilo of tomatoes, a liter of oil or a head of let-
tuce might be worth—I'll bet you did not even know the price of the
cans of condensed milk—and you have always sat down for dinner not
knowing what would be served, and without its mattering to you in the
least—it never occurred to you that it was your responsibility—
whether, depending on the cook of the moment, it was a delicious and
even sophisticated meal or pure rubbish, without its mattering if on
Christmas day my father, my brother and I found ourselves improvis-
ing some kind of sandwich in the kitchen: I am afraid that to you eating
seemed like a servitude, a vulgar necessity, and you would not have hes-
itated to replace meals with pills), and until recently when you let ev-

erything fall into a state of complete neglect, which my brother literally cannot stand, to washing your stockings and underpants in the sink every night and hanging them on the towel rack to dry. Two activities that are perhaps full of great symbolic significance, but that took you little time. I have known many cases of wasted talents, of drive that came to nothing, especially the talents and drives of women, especially women of your social class and generation, but of all of them you really take the cake, maybe because you would never accept substitutes or alternatives: I mean that the idea never even crossed your mind to open a gift shop or a store for infants' wear; you would have liked to be an architect, an interior designer, a painter, and we will never know how far you would have gone if you had been born a man.

So in the intense and limited world of my childhood there reigned the conviction that whatever you did—which at some point I began to suspect was very little—you did better than anyone. (The demand for perfection and the prohibition against lying, no matter what the circumstances, were points on which you and Papa, both so puritanical—so agnostic but so puritanical—agreed—although he, more modest, would not have used the term "perfection" but rather "a job well done"—without having to consult beforehand any manual whatsoever, and if the first of these conditioned us greatly, for better or for worse, it now seems to me more for better than for worse, the second brought upon us a heap of grotesque and awkward situations, a heap of absurd calamities.) But you also had your own peculiar and very typical way of doing things, and you have always enjoyed, and maybe that's why I too have enjoyed—one of so many inherited and shared tastes—small transgressions. Do you remember that at my brother's first Holy Communion, when all the mothers—there had to be a way of distinguishing the ladies from the other women—were wearing hats, you (so unhispanic and so unreligious, because you believed, or pretended to believe, in fairies, in nymphs of the streams, in mischievous gnomes who damaged or concealed household objects, even, if you really press me, in ghosts—you have not lost your mind lately, contrary to what my brother thinks, and I suspect you are having long conversations with your father, who has been dead for more than sixty years—but not in the severe and boring and repressive god of the Christians, perhaps a bit more in the beautiful gods of Greek mythology—you always confused aesthetics with ethics, or favored the first to the detriment of the second: do you remember having often told the story of Phryne,* who before the court who was passing judgment on the crimes of her father, took off her clothes, and her body was so beautiful that the judges [and this seemed to you reasonable] set him free?—or in the deities of Germanic mythology, passing through the dubious filter of Wagnerian opera:* yes, Mama, you knew who Siegfried was and Gunther* and what both were guilty of doing to Brunnhilde,* prototype of the spiteful, unhappily married woman, although knowing it was of no use to you) made your appearance wearing a splendid lace mantilla, to the astonishment of the audience and the enthusiasm of the priest and the prudish teachers (this was no longer the Colegio Alemán,* which had closed at the end of the Second World War), who interpreted your gesture upside down, taking as a sign of simple piety what was really the desire to shock and a piquant transgression (as for me, I was so concerned about the fact that the two of you, Papa and you, were going to take Communion without having previously confessed, an unheard-of sacrilege that could plunge you headfirst into the last circle of hell— you never bothered to explain to your children your attitude concerning religion—that I was not in the mood for trifles like mantillas and hats)?

Very elegant in your mode of attire, you did not follow to the letter the dictates of fashion, which were then very strict, but instead reclaimed elements from the past and combined them with others of your own invention that sometimes became fashionable later on: in fact, all of your clothes were magnificent and you almost never threw anything away, you kept the garments carefully, to have them reappear in a different form—that blessed mania of yours to change everything: clothing, jewelry, rooms—or in a different combination, at the proper time. You liked furs (we were years away from the time when animal lovers came up with the obvious idea that we were not allowed to wear them: that abomination of young seals being beaten to death or astrakhan fetuses snatched from their mothers' wombs), and you had coats, jackets, stoles, but they were not always the most usual furs, and in cases where they were, the unusual tailoring made them less recognizable (how you always mocked those mink coats, very full and down to the ankles, so they would last a lifetime and never go out of fashion, but for that very reason never were in fashion!). Your hats were custom-made by a refugee from some eastern European country—whose name was difficult to pronounce and impossible to remember, the owner of two magnificent and ferocious German shepherds, whom she had to confine if there were other customers but not if you and I were alone in the fitting room—following point by point the instructions that you, seated before the dressing-table mirror, the fantastic dogs lying meekly at your feet, often resting their snouts on them, often one symmetrically on either side of you, as in a Chiparus,* gave her, and that caused to appear, disappear, superimpose, group and regroup on the felt hat that covered your head, feathers of exotic birds—the fantastic feathers of birds of paradise—multicolored flowers, costume jewelry brooches and hatpins, bows of tulle, of silk, of velvet, although there were almost always few elements in the final selection.

More than twenty years ago I chanced to meet in the London airport (where on the same occasion I also came across the man who had been my first adolescent love) the daughter of your tailor—I did not recognize her, but she knew me—and she was describing the commotion in the workroom when you were coming: the tailor and the seamstresses nervous that they might not have understood what you wanted—which was always something very concrete and precise—the apprentices making up excuses to go out to the hallway and secretly peek into the fitting room, terrified and fascinated—so I was not the only one to be terrified and fascinated!—before your slender upright figure, the impeccable and personal attire, the handsome shoes almost without heels (they must have been difficult to get in those days), the beautiful, manicured hands without nail polish, the face—not exactly beautiful, but you have always stressed, and rightly so, that you were not a handsome woman—almost without makeup, and a mink coat on the shoulders, stubbornly camouflaged as some other fur (the slightest sign of ostentation was considered by my parents to be an inexcusable and common vulgarity).

And I am again surprised at your swiftness: the fact that care of your person, like any other activity you undertook, took so little time (hence the unbearable monstrosity of the slowness and clumsiness, almost disablement—although you keep trying to jump up and run from one end of the house to the other, almost always at night when the nurse is asleep, with the inevitable falls, because you have been unruly and headstrong to the end—to which illness has condemned you in your final years). Going shopping with one of my aunts, with the nanny, with the mother of a girlfriend, took an entire afternoon (and I think that deep down it did not bother them, quite the contrary, to pass the time in vain, fanciful activities, something which allowed them—but not you, you did not need this—to feel busy and useful and even to complain about having too much work) spent quarreling with the saleswomen, having them fill the counter with goods, even taken—how patient saleswomen were in those days—from the show window or the warehouse, handling them, complaining about the price, going to the door out to the street to check the exact color in the daylight, to then sometimes return home without having bought a thing and putting off the essential purchase until the following afternoon. But going shopping with you was very different, shopping with you made me giddy with delight (the pleasure was of course enhanced by the infrequency with which I did something in your company, since you supervised our education—you had sent us, despite the hand wringing of my haughty and pious grandmother and my prelate uncle, who maintained in private that he had been one of the instigators of the glorious national uprising, who thus saw their worst suspicions confirmed, to the Colegio Alemán, where there was coeducation and the only religious instruction consisted of preparatory classes for those who were going to receive First Communion; you chose conscientiously the young women who took care of us, the private teachers, the doctors, and you did everything possible, really everything humanly possible, to get me from early childhood to practice a sport, when I was hopeless in all of them—but in our childhood you devoted very little time to us).

It was a treat to accompany you to the furrier, a slight Jew who, I imagine ignoring your frivolous sympathy for the Nazis, showed you his best pieces and assured you that he would let you have them for a good price for the pleasure and above all the publicity he would gain from your showing off the garments made with them; to the renowned fashion designer where you acquired at low prices some of the outfits that were almost new, just having been displayed two or three times by the models on the catwalks, who were not then the marvel of anorexic thinness they would turn into years later, and that fit you perfectly; to the Hungarian or Polish milliner with the handsome, ferocious dogs that you liked as much for being ferocious as for being handsome, that only you could caress, and I by delegation; to your jeweler, who had fun designing with you exclusive jewelry, sometimes inspired by other pieces that we had seen or that appeared in foreign magazines, because if one could wake up in the morning at home and find the living-room furniture all changed around, or return one evening and find that a wall had disappeared or that the door to your room did not occupy its usual place and that your bed had made a hundred-eighty-degree turn, jewels too underwent in your hands, to my dismay and with the obliging collaboration of your jeweler, constant changes, so the diamonds of some earrings from your grandmother turned into an art deco brooch, or the emeralds of a bracelet into a choker, while the multiple strands of pearls, of different lusters, shapes and sizes—although your favorites were the baroque ones with a tone between ivory and pink—exhausted all possible combinations around your neck.

Going shopping with you filled me with delight: you knew exactly what you wanted and where to find it, you knew at a glance if what they were showing you was suitable, the salespeople waylaid you the minute you passed the threshold of the store, and often the owner or the manager came out to personally assist you. I do not know if it seemed normal to you that even in recently opened stores or stores you were entering for the first time, they urged you to buy whatever you wanted on credit (an offer you never accepted, because it must have violated that arbitrary but strict code that has always governed your conduct), or that they offered to send home or carry to the car trivial purchases that fit in your handbag, but I knew that that did not happen to my aunts or to almost any of the mothers of my girlfriends. And the reason is that you were for many years (the women of the FAI who chased us off were not mistaken) a great lady. And it was not that you were of better birth, because your sisters were of the same lineage and you never ever bragged about your origins (quite the opposite: you sometimes liked to shock people by talking about one of your grandfathers who had arrived in Catalonia from Andalusia* without a duro),* and Papa's family and many of the people you associated with were more aristocratic and conceited.

You were a different kind of mother and I almost always liked your being that way, although it could be trying that unusual customs reigned at home (not the least unsettling of which was that neither Papa nor you went to Mass, something absolutely unthinkable in the bourgeoisie that had won the Civil War, without ever bothering to give my brother or me, who did go to Mass on Sundays with the young woman who took care of us on the weekends, the least explanation), or that you insisted that I—a run-of-the-mill child, rather plump and with glasses before the age of three—wear my hair short in a pageboy (your French hairdresser cut it), when the other little girls without exception showed off braids or ringlets or long wavy hair (only on the day of my brother's baptism, with you still confined in bed, could one of your sisters manage to secretly curl my hair, which at that time must not have been too short), and that you devised for me, as you did for yourself, unusual clothing, a bit sportier than usual, that I suppose was extremely elegant but that made me stand out wherever I went, at a time when my greatest desire was to fit into groups and go unnoticed, and in which—it's enough to see my unhappy expression in the photographs—I died of embarrassment and irritation (I prayed to the Holy Virgin every night of one school year that it would not rain the next morning so they would not dress my brother and me up in little checked raincoats, that I do not know where the devil you had picked up and that turned me, or at least it seemed that way to me, into the laughingstock of the class; and one whole summer I stubbornly persisted in getting dirty as soon as they put it on me a white culotte with three blue stars on the front).

There were certainly times when I would have preferred a more ordinary mother, more conventional, who would at times give me some good smacks (you only gave me four slaps on the face—Papa never laid a hand on us, it was unthinkable for him—and the fact of being only four made them more terrible and unforgettable, almost emblematic, and of course you did not just give them to me arbitrarily, in a fit of impatience and bad temper that you might later regret—assuming that regret entered into your psychic makeup, which it did not—but rather because you thought they were called for, the appropriate response, just as it was fitting that a decision once made never be modified, or that a punishment never ever, for any reason, be revoked), a mother who would protect us from my father's fits of anger (which in this case there weren't any), who would side with us before teachers, before servants, before friends, even when we were not right, especially when we were not right, a mother who in our honor suspended all critical judgment, who did not apply to us the same yardstick she applied to others, and who considered us extraordinary, who devoured us with kisses (the very idea that you could eat someone up with kisses is an absurdity; not even with your son, whom you have loved and continue to love more than anyone, infinitely more than me, not even with your favorite dogs, from whom you have demanded, and of course received, a boundless loyalty and obedience, a monstrous and absolute devotion, monotheistic, have I ever seen you brimming with affection, have I ever seen you truly tender or loving; maybe, in fleeting moments, before a litter of puppies), but you were a seductive mother—all the more seductive for being distant—and I literally adored you. Papa adored you, my brother adored you, the servants—from whom you did not permit the least familiarity and whom you always kept in their place, but whom you did not meddle with at all: I do not recall your ever having dismissed a maid, they all left our home when they got married—adored you, the dressmaker and the hairdresser and the milliner and the schoolteachers all adored you, your circle of friends adored you, and the fact that your sisters and almost all of my father's family and some of the women of your group bitterly censured you only strengthened the myth.

What happened then, Mama? You often ask or ponder at what moment, at what age, I stopped loving you, and my brother stopped loving you and my children stopped loving you, because apparently all of us, you say—except my father, of course, but you do not mention him—have sooner or later stopped loving you (although you always ask when, but never why, as though it were a phenomenon caused by our malice and ingratitude or resulting from a natural and irreversible process, in any case, something that had nothing to do with you or your attitude). And maybe you are waiting for me to answer that I did in fact stop loving you at such and such a moment, or to assure you that I have never stopped loving you. And I say nothing, because I do not know the answer: I do not know at what age I stopped loving you, I do not know if I have stopped or if I ever will stop loving you. I do not know at what precise moment something went wrong in our relationship. It was inevitable that your myth, like all myths, would deteriorate—playing at being a god always entails a risk—not only because my ferocious adolescent eyes, or my lucid eyes of an adult woman, could not see you as you had been seen and wanted to be seen by the eyes of a little girl, but also because so many barren years (it is amusing that holidays irritate you and that you disapprove of the long weekends we take off from work, you who have not done any kind of work a single day of your life), so many wasted abilities, so much energy spinning its wheels and culminating in migraine headaches and attacks of nerves, have sunk you in a growing laziness and led to such a savage egoism that perhaps it is beyond egoism and one would have to invent another word for it. But if our relationship broke down, if at some point in my adolescence I confronted you and for many years did not lower my guard, it was not for something you said or did or did not do to me, nor for something you said or did or did not do to others. It was because I understood—in a sudden revelation that must have been secretly ripening for a long time within me—that never (and "never," when it relates to you, is a never without palliatives or hope), no matter how hard I tried, would I win your approval. Even if I became as elegant and seductive and as much of a lady as you were, even if I obtained what you considered to be the best of husbands, even if I had gorgeous children (tall and blond and blue-eyed, children who looked foreign), even if I surpassed your crawl and became a swimming champion, even if I wrote better than Cervantes* and painted better than Rembrandt, even if I devoted my entire life to conforming to the image of me that you had dreamed up and that must have implicitly expressed your frustrations, I would never gain your approval: I was disqualified in advance—and I am not even sure if my idolized brother was much better off in this respect— and as a result the only way to assert myself and not succumb was to stand up to you. But I discovered something even more serious and likewise irrevocable, and it was that also never, no matter how hard we tried, would you allow us to make you happy (we would never even see you content, do you know that I try to conjure up one moment when you were content, really content, when you jumped for joy, and I do not find any?). It is paradoxical that being so pleased with yourself and having so many things at your fingertips and without having the remotest idea of what could be feelings of guilt, you were not even moderately happy. (Or maybe happiness seemed to you something illusory and contemptible, reserved for fools, just as eating seemed to you a vulgarity.) And what relationship can one have, Mama, with someone who will never give us her approval and will never allow us to make her happy?

Last night I dreamed again—it happens often—that I was in your home, the home you built to your measure and where I lived the most intense years of my life, and you were also there—sitting in the green armchair where you read for hours and hours and which appears in so many of my brother's paintings, lighting a huge fire in the fireplace of the library, standing before your dressing-room wardrobe, letting me smell your perfume, showing me your mother's and your grandmother's jewels, that I liked so well and that you would mostly destroy in order to make new ones—and I am overwhelmed by so many many memories, and I think that I could have made this into a long list of mutual attacks and grievances, that I might have started this letter with the intention of settling scores, but I have discovered that the attacks and grievances have long since stopped mattering to me, that for a long time too, without being aware of it, I have lowered my guard before you, that I have accepted that not even now, on the threshold of death, do you turn to me or accept anything about me, that the story has drawn to a close, has ended, that the final curtain has come down and we are once and for all at peace.

Letter to my first love
(plain, Catholic, and sentimental)

I DO NOT KNOW WHY AFTER SUCH A LONG TIME, ALMOST HALF MY LIFE, without being in touch with you, there arose in me that spring the ever more urgent desire to see you again. There was, after the alumni dinners, gradually more and more infrequent, and the chance meetings at the opera, ever more scarce, a last fortuitous and brief encounter (I had just published my first novel which, if you brought yourself to read it, must have shocked you quite a bit, difficult for you to understand what ill-fated circumstances would have induced me to leave behind my literary babblings, the syrupy, vaguely erotic romanticism of my adolescent and youthful poems, to plunge into a lesbian adventure with such ease and verisimilitude, with such an absence of cover-ups and taboos, although you were the one who taught me to prefer Quevedo, Garcilaso and Antonio Machado* to Gabriel y Galán, Campoamor and José María Pemán,* and I had just separated from my second husband, or from my second long-term partner, if you prefer, which must have seemed to you morally reprehensible, I excluded from the choirs of the blessed for having lived in a permanent state of mortal sin, and for you it must have been the painful confirmation—painful because I believe that at no moment of your life did you stop caring about me—that for a long time I had been traveling, and without your being able to prevent it, on crooked paths, had gone astray), a chance encounter at the London airport—already on line to board for Barcelona, you accompanied by your wife and I by some women friends—about which I only recall the fervor with which you spoke about your son—it must have seemed to you a gift from the gods, you would have said from God, to have a son at your age—who, at the ripe age of four, preferred Verdi and Puccini to Wagner and Strauss,* appreciated for their true worth the ruins and ancient cities you visited (he loved Avignon),* spoke good

45

German and was the brightest child in the kindergarten; that and the disturbing impression—because at no moment of my life had I stopped caring about you—that something was not right with you, a certain stiffness in your movements, a certain sluggishness, a different coloration of the voice, although upon later asking people from the high school who saw you almost on a daily basis, no one admitted that you were ill, and although you continued with your literature classes for many years.

So I had gone many years without seeing you and without thinking too much about you, and yet never, not a single time, upon driving by the long steep stairway that leads from the avenue where the bus dropped me off to the street where the school was—prematurely torn down to build an apartment complex—had I failed to remember you, nor would I in the future; impossible to go by there without evoking the adolescent I was then, an adolescent who every morning at an ungodly hour—the Germans advocated a Spartan hygiene or moral code: get up at the crack of dawn, take cold showers in midwinter, do extremely violent physical exercise, which made gym classes and sports for me, even after leaving the timidity and fears of childhood behind, a nightmare—climbed those stairs, heart pounding, shaken by the possibility—which sometimes occurred—of meeting you, of going the rest of the way together, which filled me with happiness—genuine happiness, you know, that so fragile feeling that makes us see the world in a different way and raises the hope of touching the sky with our hands, that intoxicating happiness that is addictive and becomes, over the course of our lives, harder and harder to attain, that I have sought avidly since childhood and that I speak about in all of my novels—and made me levitate, as though touched by grace; just as it is impossible for me not to fix my gaze on the nearby church, where you took us Catholic students once a week to attend Mass, I always sitting and kneeling in a place from which I could see you, as close as possible to you, inflamed with turbulent and ambiguous fervor.

So I do not know why there arose in me that spring, mixed with fear (I was almost sixty years old and you were twenty years older than me: impossible to predict what kind of old man you had turned into, what you had been reduced to by age and the unsettling ailment that I had detected at the London airport, difficult to decide if I preferred to see you as you would be now or to keep your image as intact as possible, as well preserved as possible in my memory, as it was intact in my dreams, because I had suddenly begun dreaming about you often and carrying on with you tender, intimate conversations bathed in tears), the ardent, pressing desire to see you.

Perhaps it was because they had recently celebrated the centennial of the Colegio Alemán (which had long since gone back to being called "Alemán" and for which occasion they had constructed some splendid and expensive buildings, equipped with every imaginable facility—nothing like the old Vallcarta villa, where they even held classes in the garage and we lived in constant fear of the neighbors, we did not have a laboratory or even a library, and where I had learned so much and been so happy—and which had little by little regained the arrogant and con-ceited disposition that the Germans had temporarily lost during the years following their defeat and which made them disagreeable) and they had invited me, as a distinguished alumna, to give a lecture. And I had based my talk, ironic and nostalgic—in me nostalgia would be lethal without large doses of irony, just as my sentimentality would be intolerable without certain doses of humor—on memories of my school years, and in those memories you appeared as the central figure, resurrected from the past with a force and a vividness in part, only in part, unforeseen. Perhaps because I took for granted that you would at-tend the celebration—you could not miss my lecture—and this would afford us a privileged occasion for a reunion: the best literature student of that year had become a novelist. So that my words, as I had written them, were directed to my classmates, whom I had never lost touch with, and to our teachers at the school, but above all to you; my speech was full of very private jokes that only you could understand. Except that you, contrary to all my expectations and for the first time, did not make the date.

Maybe you felt too ill, maybe you disliked having others see you—so trim, so elegant, so self-possessed—physically diminished; maybe your relations with the governing board and even with your colleagues had not been good and you had broken off all contact with them upon your retirement, despite the fact that during the first long phase you had appeared as the principal of the school before the official organs of government, because it was an essential requirement in those days, only a few years after the end of the Second World War, which had led to the immediate closure of the Colegio Alemán and the migration of former students and teachers to other schools, and at the height of the Franco dictatorship (our Caudillo's sympathy for Hitler by that time

and for those purposes meant next to nothing), to have as a cover a
Spanish principal who supported the regime. Just as they could not
give the new school the name "Alemán" and had to rechristen it "San
Alberto Magno," and had to zealously hide the fact that it was coeduca-
tional, which in Spain continued to be a cause for scandal—my father's
conservative family stubbornly refused to understand why even in
those days they would not take me to the nuns of the Sagrado Corazón
or of Jesús María, or as a last resort to the German nuns of Santa Elizabeth*—and there were formal complaints from malicious, idle neighbors, or worthy keepers of the faith, wasn't Franco the sentinel of the
West? who must have spied on us, as I said, with field glasses from their
balconies and terrace rooves, and confirmed that boys and girls, although we were not together for recreation or almost ever on the playing field, did attend classes together, although the complaints in this regard did not thrive. Or just as they had to hide the presence among the
faculty of members of the Protestant religion, and in this case the de-
nunciations did thrive, because in those times of chiaroscuros and excesses, with the population still so divided between winners and losers,
and the clergy so prone to align itself with the former, little distinction
was made between Protestantism and any diabolical sect destined to
sacrifice babies on black altars under the sign of inverted crosses (was-
n't it absolutely certain that the infants who were sacrificed would ascend without further ado to paradise? and didn't the Protestants day by
day and deliberately offend the Virgin Mary, who was, like it or not, the
mother of God Himself and sole mediator of all graces, without whose
favor there was no salvation? and wasn't that perverse witches' sabbath
due to the fact that a satanic and lecherous priest, not content to twist
the meaning of bulls and indulgences, had fallen in love with a nun?).*
And so we were left, in the middle of the school year, without two of
our best teachers, the mathematics and the Greek teachers (neither one
nor the other had shown the slightest intent to proselytize, they might
not even have practiced the religion, but it was whispered that in the
old Colegio Alemán the Greek teacher gave gym classes in a bare T-
shirt without wearing a bra, and even showed up in this getup in the
faculty lounge whether or not the priest was there who was preparing
us for our First Communion), fired overnight and quickly replaced by
teachers of other subjects, who of course would not attempt to proselytize either, but contritely confessed that they did not know much more
mathematics or Greek than we did. All this before the helpless indigna-

tion of teachers and students. So that I on behalf of all—I was, after all, the poet of the class—seized the pen and drafted a fiery poem against Spain, fatherland that I had idolized and that had shown itself capable of such an unjust and despicable act, which could put to the test and even weaken my patriotism, and reduce my verve and enthusiasm when I would again recite—if I ever did—the lines from "El dos de mayo": "War shouted the priest before the altar with rage, war repeated the lyre in indomitable song, war cried upon awakening the people who terrifies the world, and when foreign footsteps were heard on Spanish soil, even the tombs opened clamoring for vengeance and war . . . "*

In fact, although you dedicated to it three-quarters of your life and although for years you appeared to the outside world as its principal (I never found out or have forgotten where you came from or if you had or had not been part of the Colegio Alemán), although you gave good classes—when you gave them, because often, to my despair, you were absent, or spent the hour holding forth on topics that had nothing to do with your subject—and although you cared about your students— you never missed the annual alumni dinner, nor did it occur to us to stop inviting you—I think that you never completely fit in, became a part—one sign of this was that you never bothered to learn even basic German—of the school. You, so innately Spanish (I did not have the least doubt that on the Second of May you would have run into the street brandishing a kitchen knife to confront the invading French, that you would have taken to the streets again, armed by the police if neces- sary, to combat the Marxist hordes and break the Judeo-Masonic con- spiracy—among the people I associated with, only my prelate uncle, who had written extensively on the subject, and you believed in the im- probable conspiracy—while I would presumably run "hoarse through the streets dragging the cannons" and would tell our son: "Since the fa- therland so desires, throw yourself into battle and die, your mother will avenge you").* You were not even Catalan (which allowed the Ger- mans, when they again got high-and-mighty, to benevolently regard you as middle European, halfway between the civilized culture of the North—and this showed some nerve on their part with the Holocaust so recent, which even my mother was starting to believe in—and the picturesque barbarism of the South, where the lemon tree flourished and little more), but rather of pure Andalusian stock, although not, you would explain with pride, a joking, partying, irresponsible Andalusian like some from Malaga or Seville, but rather a serious and austere and very dignified Andalusian from Cordoba,* like Seneca or Manolete.* You, a practicing Catholic (which, I reflected later, must have kept you at least until you got married in a permanent and irreconcilable state of conflict between sex and the morality which they had instilled in you and which you had assumed with all its consequences) and a sworn Falangist* (not an opportunistic militant of the eleventh hour, ready to feather his nest with the booty of the vanquished and take a privileged place among the victors, but someone who was profoundly convinced of the National Syndicalist doctrine,* one of those Falangists who were called—what wishful thinking—left-wing, who believed that the Nationalists could have avoided the execution of José Antonio* and did not do so and saw in the Franco dictatorship a betrayal of their revolutionary ideals, except that at the critical juncture, the moment of truth, one never found them on the side of the workers or the students), it was surely for this reason that you were more effective as the front man for a school where they practiced coeducation and did not require confession at all, and you could better defend their interests in Madrid. You, such a bullfighting aficionado that for years you did not miss a single fight in Las Arenas or La Monumental,* and jotted down a descriptive and critical note for each series of passes, and missed the bullfights only during the time when your mother (maybe because you were an only child and because your father had died and the two of them had made a heroic effort with their modest means to put you through the university, you had a relationship with your mother which to my way of thinking bordered on the pathological and which must have weighed heavily on your relations with other women and on the fact that you did not get married until after her death) went through a successful cataract operation, and you had promised some saint, or more likely some Virgin, such a sacrifice, but that occurred later, in the second act of our story in two acts and an epilogue. You who—as though it were not enough, to be a misfit in the school, to be Andalusian, Catholic, Falangist, and a bullfighting fan (I suppose they were unaware of your promises to the Virgin)—also often missed class (to my great distress, because your frequent cases of the flu—the Germans never caught a cold, or I either, a question of ideology—and your indispensable or perfectly dispensable trips to Madrid plunged me into the depths of despair, left my life rudderless and without purpose, why should I get up in the morning if there did not exist the possibility, not only of seeing and hearing you in class, classes that I fantasized were addressed especially to me, but even of plotting ways to bump into you in the corridors and in the schoolyard?) and were not—something which must also have seemed to the Germans, as well as to my own parents, typical of the Third World—extremely punctual. Nonetheless you were indeed punctual, besides for the bullfights, for the opera and the theater, two interests that I genuinely shared, not out of imitative zeal, just as it was not as an offering to you that I had read, by the time I took the entrance exam for the university, a large part of the works that were in the literature textbook, because during those years I continued reading as I had throughout my childhood, that is, at all hours, with an ardor and devotion and abandonment and pleasure that I would no longer experience as an adult and that I count on regaining in my old age.

On the other hand, your classes were never orthodox, and you could speak at length, at times for the entire hour, not to mention when you arrived late, on subjects that were not on the course syllabus, a syllabus that we never completed. About Andalusian girls, for instance, who danced gracefully and prettily and very chastely with a carnation in their hair at the April Fair.* And there I was—still almost as clumsy as I had been as a child—taking flamenco* dance classes—to the amazement and suspicions of my mother, who had fought tirelessly and without success to get me to practice any kind of sport or exercise—asking the cook from Almería* to teach me to dance sevillanas,* and traveling with my father to the April Fair with the ruffled dress in my suitcase (I even traveled to Switzerland and Germany with the Andalusian costume and records of the music I had learned to dance to: ambassadress of Spanish art in Europe . . .), which I did not have the chance to show off, because we did not know anyone there and no one invited us to enter the very exclusive booths or join in the festivities, and insisting on attending—I who at the newsreels closed my eyes when they showed pictures of bullfighting—a bullfight at La Maestranza,* in my zeal, in this case yes, to get close to you, to share your interests, to embody the kind of woman I imagined would please you. (For me, of as great importance as the day when the birth control pill gave me control over such important parts of my identity as my sexuality and maternity, was the day when I decided that I was not obliged to invent a new physical and mental image of myself for every new love.) So there I was, sitting with my father in two magnificent seats in the shady section that had been very difficult to get—Papa once again satisfying whims that he did not understand but respected—and returning to the hotel extremely ill

before they executed the third bull—the first had thrown the picador's*
horse head over heels, and the second had died bleeding internally and
vomiting oceans of dark blood—so sick that the trip to Granada* had
to be canceled. Luckily we had already been to Cordoba, and I had ex-
plored the city, your city, night and day, with fervor and devotion, I was
treading on sacred ground, and I had written a sonnet to the statue of
Manolete (this was before my experience with the bulls), located in the
center of a small square, which ended, "you were sad and lonely, you
were silent and cold, I kissed you on the eyes and stole from you a
flower," to which you would respond years later, halfway through the
second act of our story, with another poem: "No one crosses the square
or disturbs his silence. All is peace and quiet and stillness and repose.
Only you, light and graceful, in your early verses, arrive once more
across the square."*

So we had to leave for another occasion the Alhambra and the Generalife and the Albaicín,* and I spent the whole return trip by sea from
Cádiz to Barcelona* vomiting in the cabin, although my diet was limited to water and orange juice. And no way would I ever repeat the experience, although you argued that I had had the wrong impression,
that it was not just a question of the blood and death that I had seen,
which had been bad luck, that no one loved the bulls as much as bullfighting aficionados, that everything was designed to minimize the animal's suffering and that there was no death more noble. And a long
time later you would stress this idea in a letter: "I know how much you
hate bullfighting. And yet, if you had seen Ordóñez fighting yesterday,
I suspect you would have changed your mind, at least a little! Bullfighting journalists have said that some toreros fight like the angels. I do not
know if angels fight bulls, but if they do it is certain that they must im-
itate yesterday's bullfight of Antonio Ordóñez."*

So you could spend the class hour talking about themes that had little or nothing to do with your subject (as I said, we had never covered
the entire syllabus by the time of the final exams, so we had to memorize the last lessons at home), and you were an absolute believer in the
sacred values of religion, fatherland, and family, you believed, in the
words of José Antonio, that Spain had a unique destiny which was universal, that man was the bearer of eternal values, that Franco—although he had to a certain degree betrayed your national syndicalist
revolution—was the sentinel of the West, that to be Spanish was one of
the few important things that one could be in the world—the Germans

of course would not have agreed, not even at that time when the military defeat had made them more humble and likable, before they went back to believing with a fervor similar to yours that to be German was the most important thing one could be in the world—that our women were the most beautiful, at once the most decent and the most passionate, who when they kissed really meant it, and our men were the most gallant and brave, and if the Reds had not stolen our gold and taken it off to Moscow, depriving us of the means to acquire modern armaments, our army would also have been the best in the world, as were our police, our cinema, our literature, and our fire department, although it is only fair to say that in those days, in the early fifties, I, the majority of Spaniards who had won the war and even my parents—in other respects so critical—to a large extent shared these beliefs. And at this point, I think the time has come to confess that in those days I was really an affected prude.

All in all, I think you came close to epitomizing, even outwardly, in your demeanor and your conduct, the typical Spaniard imagined by foreigners. You were, and I know you continued to be right up to the end, chivalrous and gallant and flirtatious with women, in a way that, not just now, when it would be regarded as a museum piece, but even then, at least in Catalonia, seemed a bit old-fashioned and out of place, which would have provoked the merciless sarcasm of my mother, but which fascinated me: you behaved like a witty and refined beau, and I played brilliantly the part of the young ingénue (years later, in the second act, you would often call me "my little girl"), but not without a certain flair and cunning, as though we were both out of a one-act farce by the brothers Alvarez Quintero* which, instead of taking place on an Andalusian patio, unfolded in the courtyard and classrooms of a Catalonian-German school. You were, and must also have been until age and infirmity overcame you—assuming they did—one of those individuals who makes you feel at every moment, without rest or pause—and I do not know if I would now find it a bit exhausting—a woman, and as such, protected and revered: you would never allow us to pay for a cup of coffee, open a car door, serve ourselves water or wine. You were one of the few men, rare birds if ever there were, who truly like women, not just to sleep with (although I insist, I have sometimes wondered how you, like millions of other Spaniards, resolved the conflict between sex and religious beliefs, between erotic impulses and the almost sacred respect for woman), but to be with, to talk with: one of the few men who did not feel particularly inclined, even to discuss politics or bulls, to all-male gatherings.

But if I was fascinated by your affected and literary flirtations and your meaningful looks and your tender and slightly ironic smiles or by your taking me by the elbow to help me up the stairs (men like you generally treat us as though we were halfway invalid or made of glass) or casually laying a hand on my arm or my hair (which left me literally breathless, on the brink of asphyxiation or collapse), all of this had a price: the fear that the gestures you made with me were equal or very similar to those you made with other girl students (so obvious that besides enjoying being with women and chatting with women and gazing at us in a special way, you liked—within the most proper and decent bounds, and always in the presence of other people—to lay your hands on us). Which made me furious, not so much out of real jealousy as from the suspicion that I might not be something special for you, that it might be all in vain, the care with which I put on every morning a different dress—never in my life had I bought, or would I again buy, so much clothing, washed my hair with egg yolk and rinsed it with chamomile tea, to let it fall very blond over my shoulders or gather it into a ponytail (I have already said that with each new love, and this was my first love, I invented another image of myself, and I will now add that if I have often heard other women say that they do not get all decked out for others but rather for themselves, I have only tried to make myself beautiful for a particular person, who of course is not I), and even came close to putting (my mother, half witch that she was who did not miss a single detail, was already more than suspicious about my relationship with the literature teacher, and had hastened to comment on how ugly his teeth were and had begun, something completely new, prying into my correspondence in the summer) a double carnation in my hair, and too young at the age of fifteen to wear makeup, smeared my eyelids with my father's blue cream, which I believed made my eyelashes stand out like mascara but which must have just made them sticky (until a girlfriend asked me in all innocence what disease I had in the eyes). The suspicion that so many stratagems and so much lingering on the stairs to the street, so much maneuvering to sit near you in church, so much pretending to bump into you in the corridors and in the schoolyard, and having learned to dance acceptable sevillanas and even a fandango,* so much irritating my family and the neighbors practicing the castanets (I called them "palillos" or "postizas"* because it sounded more gypsylike), having learned by heart almost the entire poetic works of Bécquer* and having read in its entirety, from the first line to the last, the *Episodios Nacionales,** and even having attempted to like bullfighting; the suspicion that so much effort and devotion could have led to nothing, could have fallen into a void without echo or response, the whole story unfolding only in my head, the premonition perhaps that love could at times be a solitary game.

And these thoughts filled me with such anguish, with such burning rage, that on one occasion—you must have talked too much to a female classmate or teacher, showed too great an interest in her affairs, or looked at her in a way that seemed to me special, or took her hand or grazed her hair—far from dissuading them, I had encouraged my classmates to put a firecracker in your desk, and it went off with a tremendous bang in the middle of the class, scarcely a meter away from you, and the windows shook and we jumped in our seats, despite having been forewarned of what was going to happen—although we did not suspect, or at least I did not suspect, that the explosion would be so terrible—but you—and I did not take my eyes off you for a second—remained unperturbed, just an almost imperceptible gesture of surprise, which left us speechless with admiration and greatly enhanced your prestige, augmented by the unusual fact that you did not impose on us any punishment, and resumed the class without comment at the exact point where it had been interrupted a few seconds earlier—a gesture which two other Cordobans would doubtless have emulated: Seneca and Manolete—because in those days I still admired—maybe in part from my mother's influence, but also because it was in the air we breathed, they were heroic years—physical courage, especially in men, and I believed, because it was what I had been told, that the act of Guzmán el Bueno,* hurling his dagger to the Arabs who held him under siege so they could use it to assassinate his own son before his very eyes, or that of General Moscardó,* several centuries later but so similar, allowing the Reds to kill his son rather than surrender the alcazar (ye gods, how they harped on those two stories, and the one about the Spartan child,* so brave that he let the baby fox that he was hiding under his tunic tear open his chest and take his life, rather than let them find it), were both, that of Guzmán el Bueno and that of General Moscardó, magnificent and heroic and worthy of being taken as a model, and that we women of virtue—virginal and impassioned—should also run around until our breath failed us calling men to arms or

firing them from the ramparts of Saragossa (it's no wonder that the Pilarica* said she did not want to be French), and bravely ordering our
sons (assuming they were the fruit of holy matrimony) to their deaths,
the most beautiful girls ready to smile, at the proper time, upon the
bravest of conquerors (weren't all men supposed to be courageous?
didn't it say in the military passbook, after the question "Valor?" the
answer "Assumed"?). And if we add that you were extremely generous—with your money and your time—and extremely proud ("stolz
wie ein Spanier"),* I think you did indeed come close to embodying the
stereotype that foreigners ("the blond barbarians of the North," the
publisher Carlos Barral* would say, priding himself on not knowing
English) had of the Spanish gentleman.

For three years I had you as my literature teacher, and for three
years I was in love with you, at the end of which time there were two
magical moments, the kind that life doles out sparingly, and that
should, they say, parade before our eyes at the moment of our death.
Although I have later experienced great loves, feverish passions, raving
ecstasies in which I believed I could touch the sky with my hands, although I have been happy beyond measure and have plunged into the
most absolute despair (reality always deformed and magnified by literature), nothing has ever dimmed those moments. Both occurred in the
chaotic, permissive atmosphere that reigns in the schools—and in ours
more than others—once the exams are over. One took place at the end-
of-the-year party, which began when the children had already left and
the only ones remaining were the upper-class students, teachers,
alumni, families and friends. There were sandwiches on black bread
with horseradish and all kinds of cold cuts, frankfurters, homemade
cheesecakes, fruitcakes, chocolate cakes. And there was music and
dancing and alcohol until the wee hours of the morning. I suspect that
the neighbors who spied on us suspiciously and virtuously from the
rooftops, windows and balconies (some of the party took place in the
garden) must have felt, then more than any other time, scandalized, because it was obvious that no one was controlling the consumption of alcohol, and there were, both inside and outside the building, a multitude of dark corners where couples were concealed, all this during
years when parties in friends' homes—perhaps less so at parties in my
home, my parents almost always being more permissive—the inde-
scribable bashes, were presided over by a big jar of diluted sangria and
another of orange juice, the lights were on at all times, and at least one

of the mothers, almost always the lady of the house, sat with us in the living room, to make sure that the embrace allowed in the slow dances was not tighter than was proper, and to call the girls to order if that occurred and forbid them from dancing again with such and such a boy. You must remember that in those years—when theoretically one was supposed to sunbathe with a bathrobe on—to the priests dancing was always a sin, so even those prudish parties were a cause for scandal.

But the night of the end-of-the-year party—of my last year of high school—I did not let myself be drawn by anyone into the shadiest corners of the garden or the dark, empty classrooms, and I only drank Coca-Cola, yet that night I was as if touched by grace, glowing from within. I danced all the dances, I smiled and flirted with this one and that, and I even allowed the most handsome and sought-after boy at the party, who after a first dance would not let me go, to hold me a little more tightly than the norm and bury his nose in my hair. (That night I did something that has always annoyed me: to arouse boys only to then beat a retreat, with a grotesque "What were you thinking? Whom do you take me for?", but I will say on my own behalf that what I presumed to be indecent was not, even that night, so far removed from the naughty and very chaste heroines of the brothers Alvarez Quintero, and was part of the game played by all.) But I only danced, smiled, flirted and allowed others to squeeze me a little and sniff my hair in your honor: it was with you that I would have gone not to a dark corner, but to the ends of the earth, and would have allowed you to think whatever you wanted and take me for whatever you chose. And you were observing me from far or near and always with a vague smile on your lips, throughout the night. And very late, around three in the morning, when my parents were about to pick me up, you finally asked me to dance with you, to dance a "paso doble"* (there is no more Spanish dance, and you were not going to ask me to dance some "sevillanas"). And they were three minutes of ecstasy.

The second magical moment took place the following morning. We were all walking around, teachers and students, with nothing in particular to do except gather up our belongings, say goodbye, exchange summer addresses. And I do not remember how the subject of the Gothic quarter* came up, and I confessed that I had never been there. And leaving me on the brink of collapse, you offered to take me there that very instant. We went by taxi to the cathedral, and I walked by your side through the old quarter of Barcelona (I fearing that you would discover my levitation, that you would notice that I was walking beside you several inches in the air, without my feet once touching the ground; and both of us with that special fear, that extreme caution, that makes us ever careful not to touch, not to allow ourselves even the slightest brush, because touching each other is precisely what we are longing for with all our body and all our soul), marking the route with indelible signs that would remain with us as long as we lived, so that even today (just as when I go by the school stairway or the church) I cannot walk there a single time, even when I am in a hurry, even when I am in company, without remembering you, without looking with special tenderness at the exquisite balcony situated in the angle between two walls, which made us think of the one where Juliet appeared and Romeo climbed up. But the supreme ecstasy, for me hitherto unknown, occurred a little later, when the two of us were alone in the cloister of San Pablo.* There, for the briefest space of time—so brief that there remained the doubt as to whether it had really happened or I had imagined it—you brushed my cheek and my hair with your lips, in something that much resembled a kiss. And that very night I would write an inspired poem entitled "In the cloister of a sanctuary," which said among other beauties: "Neither lilting river, nor sweet nightingale, filled with notes the morning fair; only silence, eternal troubadour, charmed us with his wingèd air . . . The cloister was solitary and concealed, with its fine columns' lofty ways; the ancient walls of the sanctuary conserve the ardor of their/your gaze."* If you also wrote a sonnet that night—you knew that the sonnet was my favorite poetic form and you handled the verses much better than I did—on the same momentous event, it has never come into my hands.

And then? After that blazing and promising first act finale? Then five years went by, my college years, which at the age I was then was a heap of time. With the thirty-six or thirty-seven years old you were when we stopped seeing each other you were already an adult, I would even venture to say a man of mature years, whereas I, from the age of seventeen to twenty-two, had gone from being an adolescent to an adult woman (as for maturity, in my case I would prefer not to discuss it). Perhaps too much time had passed to allow us to bring to a happy ending the matter that was pending between the two of us. I had completed, or almost, my degree in humanities (not majoring in Spanish literature, as everyone who had known me in high school had predicted, but rather in history, because I did not want to tie the pure and anarchic joy of reading to something that would in a sense be an obligation: it's ironic that I ended up running a publishing house and have to wait until retirement to again read at random and for sheer pleasure). And I had been a Falangist for a year (I remember proselytizing at all hours and everywhere, from the corridors of the university where my fellow students looked on in amazement, to the subways and buses full of workers, who listened to me with every imaginable suspicion), and for two years not coincidental with this, a fervent Catholic (on the point of conversing with God every night), but you had played no part in either of these conversions, although I suppose they would have delighted you, and I had renounced both by the time we again met. And during those five years I had also lived through two important love stories. (In fact I should have suspected even then, although I did not until much much later, that love had an extremely important place in my life, but that for the beautiful love story, the romantic love story that lasts until the death of the lovers, and perhaps beyond, something was needed with which I was not, never had been, endowed.)

The second act began—and the opening was as brilliant and promising as the ending of the first—when, having passed every course for my major and completed the thesis, I found myself before the stumbling block—I knew it was going to happen, but I had kept postponing the problem—that I could not obtain the degree without having passed "the three Marys"* (just as I could not get a passport without having first done social service, or get on a train without the formal written consent of my parents, or leave my family home—except to get married or enter a religious order—until coming of age, which for women was set at twenty-five years), that is: nationalist training, religion, and gymnastics. The two theoretical subjects did not constitute a problem: I memorized the questionnaire and took the tests for the remaining courses together, but gymnastics once again rose before me—I swore for the last time—as an insurmountable obstacle, and I relived the anxiety of my high school gym classes, where I had never been able to climb a rope a single inch, do a somersault without falling over, or even jump rope (I simply could not adjust my body to the rhythm imposed by the rope, just as I could not adapt my movements to those of the horse, and instead of trotting elegantly in the English style, would time and again go bouncing along like a sack of potatoes in the Spanish style: "There are more days than sausages,"* declared my horseback riding teacher to encourage me, but it seems there were not enough days, maybe because neither were there so many sausages), and I was so hopeless in ball games that not even my best friends wanted me on their team, because it was not helpful to have someone who moved around the field like an idiot and only touched the ball when it hit her on the head. There was no possible subterfuge to pass the university gym classes: it was a heap of hours, if you put together the three classes, and they were all practical courses, and the sum total made me dizzy.

So it occurred to me—although we had not seen each other for so long and had gone five years without talking to each other alone—to call you up and ask for your help. Surely your long membership in the Falangist Party and your numerous contacts could finally be of some use! (I believe this was the first and the last time that I asked for references for an exam.) And we arranged to meet at one of the beautiful old cafés full of literary tradition—at night groups of writers and theatrical people gathered there—that are inexorably vanishing, and along with them fragments of the past, from our city (perhaps your native city continued to be Cordoba, but you had been living among us for so long that although I did not consider you a Catalan, I did think of you as an Andalusian from Barcelona; wasn't I myself a Barcelonese from nowhere?). In the café, which was almost empty at that hour of the afternoon—it was not one of those places where married women went for tea—we sat down at a table by the large windows looking out on the street and watched the night falling on a gray day, more like autumn than the middle of spring, on the other side of the glass. And I guess we must have started out talking about the problem of my three pending gym classes, which you could in fact largely solve, by talking to a woman instructor who was a friend of yours and having the insurmountable number of hours reduced to an almost symbolic minimum, and then we must have asked each other politely about the most notable and least intimate events of the last five years, about our respective families—in your case, just your mother—about the alumni of my class, about our future plans. And then, after our third *cortado*,* I found myself—I knew that some day we would have to talk about it, but not that it would be that afternoon—launched on a vivisection of what I had felt for you in high school, I asked if you had known that it was love, and if you had felt a special predilection for me, or if I had just been one more student. And a smile danced on your lips and a thousand sparks lit up behind your thick-paned glasses, and you affirmed that you had indeed been aware of my love for you, that I had indeed been a very special student, that you liked me a great deal, but what could you attempt with a child who was twenty years your junior and moreover your student? But you and I pointed out—it must have been I—that I was no longer a child, nor a student, and that the twenty years separating us were now of much less importance. And we went out for a stroll, very close beneath your umbrella, and we arrived at the Gothic quarter and found our balcony in its proper place, and you took me to see the house which before the war had served as the headquarters of the Falange, and there was no longer any of the Falangist left in me, but that afternoon nothing mattered apart from us. And we kissed each other greedily in various settings moistened by the rain, as though we were trying to make up for so much lost time.

And for weeks, almost the entire summer, I believed that our relationship had a future, I thought that we were both—at last on a par—in love. Few times—only years later with Esteban—have I felt so pampered, so protected, so flattered, so fully accepted. I think that your capacity for affection and your tenderness and your generosity are extraordinary. The difference in age, the implausible fact of sharing an apartment with your mother (although I had made a good impression on her—impossible to suspect the reasons for this obvious misunderstanding, and we had spent some agreeable and picturesque evenings together, munching cookies with café con leche, seated at the round table beneath which you must have turned on a heater in the winter, in a grimy apartment you got to by climbing a stairway with no light and with loose floor tiles, and which was stuffed with furniture and knickknacks, some of which, you said and I believed you, were very valuable—Virgins, antique carvings, bell jars, small oil lamps—although those were the ones that scared me the most), the distance between two such disparate ideologies, such different lifestyles and ways of seeing things, and not even your love of bullfighting, seemed like insurmountable obstacles, or maybe the idea did not even cross my mind.

We sat at tables in the darkest cafés—empty or filled with couples so immersed in their own stories that they did not even see us—where the waiters, or so I blushingly feared, observed us a bit mockingly, but also I think with warmth (one did not often find there men as serious, as elegant, as old as you, but neither must the boys at the other tables have left such generous tips), or on some benches on Montjuic,* with the city spread at our feet and no one around us. And there we kissed and caressed each other voraciously. I imagine, and this may be only conceit on my part, that never before had your old struggle between sex and morality gotten so close to the boiling point. Burning with desire, it seemed to you the highest proof of love and respect never to reach the culmination of those savage and so tender assaults.

And one day, after one of those onslaughts that took us further than the previous ones, you finally proposed that we move somewhere where we could be alone, and I—I don't even remember why, maybe because it bothered me that my first time would take place in a house of call—put up a certain resistance which you gave in to, but the serious and unexpected thing was that the following day you congratulated me on my conduct (it was indeed at that point that you lost forever, certainly without being aware of it, the until then open possibility of taking me to bed). I just could not understand, with my twenty-two years I could not understand that you were pleased that I had said no. That presupposed that, as in the allegorical religious plays of Calderón,* human beings were divided into two parts: on the one hand the body, or the instincts, very close to those of the animals, and on the other the spirit or soul, which should repress those instincts if it did not want to stray from the path leading to paradise. I discovered in you two opposing wills, almost two different people, and while the one, blind and bedazzled, was seeking to make love to me, the other was resolutely keeping watch to make sure that did not happen. I even wondered whether, if I had acceded to your desires—it was obvious that you would not have abandoned me or stopped loving me—it would have been a little awkward for you to take me to eat cookies at the round table of your blessed mother.

That September I took a Mediterranean cruise with my parents and a group of friends, and even before the ship set sail, there was on the washstand of my modest cabin (they were austere times—at least for the bourgeoisie my parents were a part of—and although the adults traveled in first class, the young people, more as an educational principle than to economize, shared cabins in the deep belly of the ship) an overflowing, almost excessive bouquet of red roses, and attached to it, instead of a simple card, a small notebook made by hand: on the cover a collage of newspaper cutouts reproducing a small paper boat, and in blue, the words "¡Buen viaje!";* on the inside a handful of verses you had written for me. And it was charming and moving (my cabin-mate, a very young girl, looked at me in astonishment, wondering who I was and whom I had for a boyfriend), but one of the poems said: "You have the name and body of a Jewish woman, the Nazarene face of the Virgin María. You are, my beloved, Christian and pagan like Andalucía,"* and this made me aware of the insuperable distance separating the ideal woman of your dreams from the woman I was, or that I had become (I suppose that at the age of fourteen or fifteen your poem would have seemed to me simply sublime) and that was no longer going to change. Those verses could have been written to any of the girls painted by Julio Romero de Torres,* but the only resemblance they had to me (it was impossible that you not somehow suspect this) began and ended with the name. And in every port where the ship docked one or more of your letters was awaiting me, lamenting my absence, suffering for the time we were apart which was becoming interminable to you, but awaiting with great excitement my return, upon which we would do so many beautiful things together. And I wrote you from the ship (I spent many days, perhaps weeks, turning it over, but it seemed to me less difficult to write it to you than to tell you face to face, which was cowardly nonetheless) a single letter, one of those absurd, impossible letters in which you staunchly try to palliate what admits of no palliatives, to explain what requires no explanation (it would suffice to say along with the poet: "I loved you, I no longer love you, all is over"), to make bearable, in my case by means of the worst literature, a sadness that must of necessity be intense, that you lie about when you assure the other that you share, and that has no remedy other than the passage of time. And I think that the hardest thing for me, you know, what made me feel the worst, was that due to the slowness of the mail in those days, I kept receiving your love letters almost to the end of the trip, until you received mine and stopped sending them.

So I do not know why, after so many years (I wrote the letter that brought our story to an end in September of '59) of hardly seeing you and only thinking of you occasionally, that spring I felt the desire (mixed with the fear of finding out what kind of old man you had turned into and to what extent you had been ravaged by illness) to see you again. Perhaps it was because, as I told you, they celebrated the centennial of the school and you did not show up, thereby missing a splendid occasion for a reunion. Or perhaps because, upon turning sixty, there was a worsening of the nostalgia that I have dragged along like a chronic, incurable disease, with some benign and some heartbreakingly fierce moments, ever since infancy, so enormous that at times, crazy as it is, I even feel nostalgia for the bad.

It was very easy to locate you; I did not even have to ask anyone for your current address or telephone number because they were in the phone book. I called you a couple of times, at slight intervals, as though I were leaving up to chance whether or not we would meet again. On both occasions a pleasant voice, which I supposed must be that of your wife, invited me to leave a message on the answering machine, but if I did not even know what I was going to say if I got in touch with you, if I did not even know if I really wanted to get in touch with you, what the devil kind of message could I leave on the answering machine? A few days later I called a third time, expecting to hear the voice of your wife in person, not recorded, but the voice I heard was not that of your wife, and disconcerted, I asked for you. And the voice answered that you had grown up and had already entered the university. That is, they were talking about your son, who has the same name as you and whom you had told me about years earlier at the London airport. And I followed the conversation blindly, waiting for something to give me a clue, as I said to myself that it could not be your mother, who had died long before—maybe your wife's mother, or her father, because the voice had no gender? It was very strange, because the person on the other end of the line seemed to know who I was. And the voice commented that he was already eighty years old, and at first, strange as it may seem, that fact confused me still more, until suddenly I had the revelation: that hoarse, genderless voice of someone who had reached the incredible age of eighty was yours. And then I asked if you would like to see me and you answered, "Very much," and I informed you that I had just turned sixty and had also aged. And you immediately replied that that was impossible, because I would never grow old. And then all the past returned at once and overwhelmed me. Of course it was you! That voice of the gallant seducer, of the inveterate flirt, was now unmistakable! And I was again beautiful and sensual, I was at once Christian, Moor and Jewess, like the women of Julio Romero de Torres, and like them, I was immortal. Your "very much" and your "you will never grow old" made me feel better; for days they warmed my soul. And I even felt a twinge of envy toward your wife, because, although the two of you must have gone through difficult moments and although it must have been and must continue to be very hard for her—the difference in age between you is even greater than that between you and me—to endure your illness with calm and courage, she must have had by her side a man who dedicated to her a total devotion, who found her without pause or letup young and beautiful, who would repeat to her those ridiculous, flattering, tender words—those words that warm the soul—until death did you part.

What followed was a bit strange. Your wife called me one morning at the office, and asked if I was free that evening and would like to have dinner with you, because you were going to celebrate your birthday. And I answered that I was free that night and that I would love to have dinner with you on any other occasion, but that I did not want to intrude on such an intimate family affair. And she insisted that it would only be the four of us—the two of you, your son and I—and that they would be very pleased if I would accept. So you all picked me up that night in front of my house. Of course you were an old man, but as elegant and impeccable as I remembered you, whereas she, your wife, did not conform to what I had decided was your ideal woman, like the woman who would have pleased your mother; for that she obviously had too much character. Besides the four of us, there was a mutt in the car that you had picked up somewhere and could not stand to be left alone at home, so now it was jumping loose all over us, moving from the front seats to the back, without your making (and I did not recall your liking animals, although perhaps you did not dislike them, because I have known various people, including my own brother, who were animal lovers and bullfighting fans, an absurdity like any other) the slightest protest. And you took me to an unusual restaurant outside of the city where they knew you well, there were no other customers and they served us a meal as gargantuan as it was exquisite, which we all, yourself included, devoured with shameless pleasure. I liked your wife and your son (the free-and-easy affection she lavished on you seemed to me to a certain extent understandable, but it seemed unusual that a young man like your son would be so attentive to you and in such a natural way: he knew at what exact moments you would need help and hastened to offer it to you with surprising effectiveness). I was very glad to see that in the end you had fallen into good hands, and not into untrustworthy hands like mine. And on the way back in the car, you and I finally began to reminisce about school days, to exchange news about other students from my class. And although the number of students who had gone through your classroom in such a long teaching career must have been legion, you recalled without apparent effort the name and circumstances of almost all of them. And in the backseat where the two of us were sitting—your wife was at the steering wheel, and your son, by her side, was trying to prevent the dog from landing on us so often and with such force or when changing gears—was set up a certain complicity, a conversation that could approximate to those that had appeared for the last few months in my dreams. And I told myself that, if there was not time now, because we immediately arrived at my home, there would be many other occasions to review our story and construct a suitable epilogue.

So we agreed that, after finishing my summer vacation a week or two later and returning to the city, the four of us would have dinner together, this time at my home. And I was considering what would be the best day and the most suitable menu, something that you would like—I had seen that your family appreciated good cooking—but that would not cause you too many problems, when, upon returning one evening from the seashore, they told me that your wife had called to inform me that you had died—suddenly and unexpectedly, from a heart attack that had nothing to do with your illness and that had occurred without the slightest warning—the night before. It was strange to recover you after so many years to then lose you again at once and forever. Life—isn't death by chance another side of life?—had given our story, and without my consent, the most final of epilogues.

Letter to Eduardo
(dialogues in the shadows)

THE LAST NEWS I HAD OF YOU WAS A LETTER FROM ONE OF YOUR FRIENDS and colleagues in Buenos Aires, in October five or six years ago, in response to one of mine that never reached you. "The reason for Eduardo's silence," it says, "is the heartbreaking fact of his death, which occurred last June 3rd, due to a sudden lethal cancer that appeared in the liver and then spread to the right lung. When he arrived in Paris they had to hospitalize him, and after undergoing tests that revealed the seriousness of the disease, we brought him back to Argentina, where he only survived a couple of weeks. I was at his side when he passed away peacefully"; and further on: "I am confiding these things to you because since Eduardo called you, thereby renewing a friendship of your young years, you have joined those of us who constituted his only family. Your novels were the admired reading of our publishing house clan, Eduardo's true home. In one of his suitcases was a copy of *Mis dos vidas* by Berta Singerman* (the cause of the renewal of your friendship), dedicated by her to you." I know that at that time I could have easily obtained a lot of information about your life—so complex and so contradictory and so uneven, a puzzle with many pieces missing that now I will never be able to assemble, no matter how hard I try, too late, to delve into the past—and your death, so tragic (or maybe not too much so, if you died, as your friend assures me, peacefully—"death," you said in one of your works, "is not in the eyes of the one who lives it, but of the one who beholds it"—and surrounded with people who loved you—it was easy to love you, it was always very easy for all of us to love you, and it may well be typical of you, of your contradictory character, to raise hell about the smallest trifle, to feel sorry for yourself over the slightest thing, and then to confront death with fortitude), so tragic then, and without doubt unexpected, just a few days before our reunion (so few that, if you had not at the last minute changed the itinerary of the trip and had gone first, as was your original plan, to Barcelona, we still would have had the chance to see each other), when you assured me that this reunion was the main reason for your coming to Europe. "The main reason for this trip was our reunion," you write, with a still steady hand, from the Paris hospital, and "As soon as my temperature goes down, I will write you at length. Now I am afraid the nurses and doctors will scold me. In any case, I have not given up hope of seeing you."

So many years without hearing from you, and then to lose you when I was just on the brink of finding you again! It was certainly due to pure chance, and I have not read or heard tell from anyone else of similar experiences, but with me this recovery of something or someone long lost, to then immediately lose him again beyond recall, has happened repeatedly, and not just in your case and that of the literature teacher who was my romantic and fanciful first love, whom I think I never told you about, partly because by my second year at the university—that is, between the first and the second acts of that story—I had almost stopped thinking of him, and partly because you and I talked a great deal, for hours and hours, during our brief and passionate relationship, but almost exclusively of you. We spoke of your, of our existential anguish (Sartre, Camus, Juliette Greco);* of your wide range of fears, that I understood and in part, only in part, shared; of the constant strain because of money problems, the sordidness of which disturbed me and which you accused me at times, and justifiably so, of not understanding or sharing enough; of your troubled and claustrophobic relationship—aggravated by the fact that for economic reasons you were compelled for a long time to live in your family home—with your father, a poor fellow, certainly a good man (in the edition of *La casa oscura** which you had dedicated to me since we met, the dedication would finally read: "TO YOU, FATHER," and the use of capital letters prevented me from knowing for sure if it was a question of the Eternal Father or your earthly father, and for which of the two you had divested me of something that I considered to be mine), and with your wicked stepmother, half a witch, who recalled the evil characters in children's stories (like so many stepmothers in children's literature, she detested her stepchildren—in this case, her only stepchild, which concentrated still more her fury—she bewitched them, transformed them into animals, accused them unjustly of abominable imaginary crimes, caused a rift with

their nearest of kin, convinced her husband to abandon them as food
for the beasts in the deepest part of the forest: closer to the mother of
Thumbelina than the witch of *Hansel and Gretel* or the stepmother of
Snow White,* or was there a buried erotic drive that made you resemble
Hippolytus* or the chaste Joseph,* against a much seedier background
that had nothing literary about it?), naïve and childlike as you were, despite your malice and your wicked ways. ("I truly believe," you say in
one of your last letters, "that we should meet. I will not allow to totter
such an important part of my ingenuousness. Because in me innocence
has always remained alive, even amid the greatest madness. It is there,
as real as you.") We discussed your murky relationship with a much
older woman, the owner of a notions store in your neighborhood,
which you assured me was not satisfactory, in any case more distressing
than pleasant—as sordid, I thought, as your constant money problems,
and I later surmised that the two sordid things were not unrelated—but
which, much as you resolved to do it a thousand times and were urged
to by Father Arturo, you did not dare to break off, or did not know how
to do it, or never found the right moment. We also talked about your
equivocal relations with other men, with other boys, not to my way of
thinking necessarily sordid (once I heard a priest say in a Sunday sermon—much of my faith foundered from listening to Sunday ser-
mons—that sin did not consist in dirtiness but rather in disorder, so it
was permissible to engage in all kinds of filth, all kinds of ugliness, but
not to change an order established by God or by humans, and I had
known at once that my place was in the camp of the clean, the disor-
derly and rebellious, and while your relationship with the shopkeeper
seemed to me dirty and ugly and murky at the source, your relations
with other men did not inspire the same repulsion), relations which
you felt—I do not know why, given the fact that my ignorance in that
domain was enormous, and that neither my advice nor my approval
would have been of much use to you—impelled to tell me about, but
which you always explained through insinuations or elaborate ellipses,
much better understood by me, I think, than you assumed. And above
all we discussed your work, that which you had already written and that
which you were going to write in the future, which, beyond all anxieties
and fears and meanness, lifted you, lifted us both, to the very stars. And
do you know something, Eduardo? Can you believe that after so many
years, and having known so many writers, celebrated or unknown,
there is not one whose talent I have believed in as I believed in yours?

Yes, when your death was still recent I could have learned much more about your life and your death, because soon afterwards one of your friends from Buenos Aires came to Barcelona—I do not recall if it was the same one who had informed me by letter of your demise, nor whether or not he revealed having been something more than a friend to you—and visited me at home, I imagine expecting to talk long and hard about you (I am sure that just as many pieces were missing in his puzzle as in mine, but not exactly the same ones, so that by joining information and forces, maybe we could have managed to almost complete the puzzle) and hoping to meet the author of the trilogy about the sea, but these expectations were dashed, because (it was not one of the most peaceful and happy periods of my life, of course, but I now think that it could not only have been due to this, nor have been the fruit of chance, but that above all it obeyed an intense and inexplicable desire not to find out, not to know) I received him like a zombie, over-drugged—who knows what explosive cocktail I must have devised and ingested, what unusual and creative blend of tranquilizers, antidepressants, marijuana, sleeping pills and alcohol—having just gotten out of bed without emerging from my stupor, to open the door staggering, sit him down beside me on the sofa and let him carry on alone, in a monologue with no interlocutor, without my even halfway understanding what he was explaining to me and entirely incapable of giving minimally coherent answers. Since then I have deeply regretted it, not so much because of the disappointment the poor guy must have felt, so fine, so good-natured, so warm, who upon his return to Buenos Aires must not have known what to report about our pathetic encounter— and who of course did not get in touch with me again—as for having missed a unique opportunity to gather information about you, to talk about you at length with someone who had probably also loved you. At that moment, Lord knows for what reasons, I did not want to find out anything, and now that it is too late I would like to know everything.

However, I had a second chance a few years ago, during a visit to Berta Singerman's home. I had never gone to Buenos Aires without dropping in to greet her, without taking her the most beautiful roses I could find in the city, faithful to what has been one of the great passions of my life, which began when at the age of fourteen my mother—who was not of course the best of mothers, who often did not even behave as you would expect of a mother, but who, if she did not pass on to me her ideas or her disposition, did pass on, perhaps without ardently intend-

ing to, the love of animals, of books, of the sea, of beautiful objects—
took me to hear her, at the first recital she gave here after our war—
which, by the way, I still thought had been started by the Reds and
which I still believed, like a large part of the youth of my generation
and social class, we had won—and during the intermission I ran to the
box office and got tickets for all her performances, and for years afterwards I followed her on all or almost all of her tours of Spain—to Pamplona, to San Sebastián, to Madrid, to Tarragona*—a passion that has
brought me huge amounts of happiness, has given me moments of ecstasy (even today, so many years later, I need only concentrate and close
my eyes to hear her recite one of her poems from beginning to end),
and that I have never tried to pass on or discuss with others, because
Berta is, always has been, but more so with the passing years, like much
of the best Argentine art and the best French art, on a fine line, a pre-
carious tightrope act separating the sublime from the vulgar, the
grotesque from the brilliant, and the spectator inevitably sees her on
one side or the other of this dividing line—to remain neutral about her
is impossible—and defending or explaining or attempting to share
what hearing Berta Singerman aroused in me would be like trying to
justify and explain and share my love of the sea or my regard for animals, something completely futile, a sorry waste of time. And you, of
course, came down on the side of a wholehearted passion. If this were
not the case, you would not have helped her write her memoirs or have
put them out from your publishing house. Now I will never know—
and it would have been so easy to ask!—how the two of you got in
touch, who came up with the idea of the book, if she harbored hopes of
the project and someone directed her to you, if the idea occurred to
you and you proposed it to her, if you were already friends—I know
that you were not when you still lived in Spain—and the idea arose
when the two of you were talking. What a magnificent Helen she
would have been! The best imaginable Helen, no doubt better than I—
who, on the other hand, never got to play that role—as though the
work had been made to order, tailored to her enormity, her excesses,
her way of overacting, her prodigious voice, and perhaps for Berta you
would have come to write the monologue that, despite promising and
talking to me about it so many times, you never came to write for me,
and that would have levitated, no doubt, between the grotesque and the
brilliant, as though genius were just one more step in the same direction, another turn of the screw. But—oh what sadness, still today, oh

what sadness—you never became Lorca* nor did I become la Xirgu,*
and not because we failed in the endeavor, but because we never even
attempted it. (At what exact or indeterminate, conscious or unconscious moment of your life—if it occurred—did you give up the idea of
writing? At what moment or in what long series of moments, indeterminate and unconscious—and it still takes my breath away when the
curtain goes up, I still burst into tears when the applause breaks out and
for some inexplicable reason I find myself in the orchestra seats and not
on the stage—did I give up becoming an actress, or put it off for so long
that the postponement in itself became an abdication?)

So a few years ago, a Singerman who was incredibly well preserved
for her age—when I met her she was already an older woman and forty
years had passed since then—impeccably groomed and made up from
the moment she left her room, still in a way seductive and fascinating,
still endowed with a robust personality, but at the same time a Singerman who—after a long life of being protected and pampered and ca-
joled, even spoiled, a life in which it was taken for granted that the
whole world revolved around her, sheltered as much as possible from
the unpleasant, tedious facets of daily life, from the most somber aspects of existence, surrounded by family, friends and admirers—had
had the misfortune of surviving—her husband, her only daughter, her
sister Paulina, so many others—and remained alone, in that apartment
that was too big, too ostentatious, too much designed to be the show-
case of a diva, mentioned that one of the members of your publishing
house—a warm, sensitive and charming young man: now I will surely
never know, among so many other unknowns, if he was the same one
who had informed me of your death by letter and visited me later at my
home in Barcelona—went to see her often, accompanied her to the
movies and the theater, took her shopping or for a walk. Why didn't I
ask him at that time for his phone number or address; why didn't I at
least make the effort to memorize his name? It must have been because
I thought there was plenty of time, that there would be other occasions;
I could not predict that I would never again see Berta, that on my next
trip to Buenos Aires, after finding her new telephone number in the di-
rectory, a phone number that was with an unknown address (so she no
longer lived in the apartment that was too big, luxurious and extrava-
gant for a woman living alone, where I had visited her several times), I
would call a bunch of times, only to hear a neutral and opaque female
voice, more and more odious with every call although it was the same

recorded message, informing me that I had reached such-and-such a number and that if I wished to leave a message I could do so after the tone; I could not predict that I would call one and a thousand times, at all hours of the day and night, and would leave messages that were gradually more hysterical and desperate, more threatening, having lost the last shred of composure, leaving my name and the name of my hotel and room number, all without response, and that, just before getting on the plane that would take me back to my city—unable to remember the name of Berta's son-in-law, the only person I knew who could have given me reliable information, and thus not knowing if she was still alive, if she had gotten senile, if they had confined her in an old people's home or a hospital, or had installed her in a smaller apartment with a companion or a nurse who did not deign or did not have orders to listen to and answer the phone messages—I sent her a bouquet of roses, I suppose the last, separated by more than forty years from the first, which I had sent as an adolescent with an impassioned note to her hotel after hearing her first recital.

By a series of improbable coincidences, two of the great passions of my life (the one I felt for you, already distant in time; and the one for Berta, which goes even farther back—I met her at the age of fourteen; you, at the age of eighteen—but from then on never until very recently interrupted) coincided a few months before your death. When I got on the phone—they had told me it was a call from Buenos Aires—I thought it must be one of so many Argentine friends, in exile here for a while and then having returned to their homeland, but it was you. You first said your name, and then, "We were friends at the university, remember?" And I, unable to believe what was happening, astonished to hear your voice after such a long time—I did not even know if you were still alive, nor did I have the remotest idea that you had finally settled in Argentina, because I had received your last letter, ages before, from a novitiate in Bolivia—dumbfounded moreover by the unheard-of stupidity of your words, of that absurd question: "Of course I remember you, of course I know who you are! How could I forget you? And what on earth made you introduce yourself as a college friend?" And I laughed, amused, very content, really content, and you also laughed, regaining our confidence and warmth as though the years had melted away, but no, I am expressing it wrong, with a confidence and abandonment and freedom that we did not have in the past; it almost seemed as though we had grown into adults, that we had, miracle of miracles, matured, that you had stopped being the perpetual child and I the stale adolescent. And you told me that you were living in Buenos Aires, that you had set up a small publishing house with some friends, that you had just published an autobiography of Berta Singerman—which you had helped her write—and that upon asking her for the names of friends who could help launch the book in Spain, she had given you a list which, to your amazement, included my name; you were sure that Berta had never spoken to you about me and you did not recall my ever having mentioned this relationship. And I answered that Berta must not have alluded to me because, despite the fact that we had become friends and that she felt a certain affection for me, I was not important in her life, in either of her two lives, as she had been in mine; a relationship that was, like so many others, asymmetrical. And I was tempted to add, but I did not want you to take as a reproach what would simply have been an observation, that if I had not said anything to you about her, it must have been because in our conversations the two of us hardly ever talked about me, only about your misfortunes, your fears and your less frequent joys, about how to solve your problems.

Several letters followed this telephone call—the last letter the one from the Paris hospital—and in the first, written on the same day as the phone call, you say: "I have just heard your voice, so distant and so near. I am overwhelmed . . . Would it be possible for me to analyze with objectivity my feelings then, my feelings now, those I have had at different times with regard to you? How to recover things as they were, without the appendices of time, the fear, the guilt, the loneliness and the shared joys? Why has there suddenly awakened in me the longing for my city, when scarcely two years ago I strolled like a sleepwalker through its streets, as alien to me as were those of Paris, London or Rome?" and further on: "When all this confusion has passed, I will tell you about the role chance has played in my life. For the time being let it just follow the course of the rejuvenation I feel today."

And it is what you call the "accidents of your life" that I fear I will never come to know. How did you wind up at the seminary of Cochabamba,* on the other side of the world, instead of entering the one in Barcelona, if you had decided to become a priest? And assuming it was not a question of a romantic outburst of solidarity with the dispossessed of the Third World—which was not unthinkable in you—what were you fleeing or what did they want to separate you from? (The plural is a euphemism, a fraud, because what I really think is: what or

whom did Father Arturo want to separate you from? And in the series
of events that I am trying to reconstruct at all costs and against all odds,
in the puzzle that I will not manage to assemble, this priest—who had
great importance in our story, who played a fundamental part—is the
piece that is most shady, most ambiguous, most difficult to place, so
frail is the outline and so blurred the color.) Were you ordained in Bolivia or did you once again leave on the run? And in relation to this, a
question that is crucial to understanding you: Did you drag along
through your entire life the dead weight (you would certainly not have
said "drag," nor would you have used the phrase "dead weight") of your
troubled and morbid and at times exalted, almost mystical, religiosity,
which Father Arturo relied on and in which your desire for security undoubtedly played an important part, but which was by no means a
sham? Did you have (in one of your letters you declare, surely in response to a comment I made about my relationship with them, so special and gratifying, and about my inability on the other hand—an idea
which you would not accept—to maintain a reasonably happy and lasting love relationship, "having had the experience of fatherhood and its
tender, at times terribly painful, complications") children? And if this
was so, assuming you did not lie or fantasize about it, with whom did
you have them and what had become of them? And how did you end up
in Argentina, and how did you come up with the idea of starting a publishing house, and where did you get the money (a little strange my curiosity about this, but money was always a determining factor in your
vicissitudes, compelling you to establish dark dependency relationships, although it was difficult for me—and this was the greatest of
your reproaches—to understand it, perhaps because I have always had
more than enough, without ever having done anything for it), and in
the second and last stage of your life who were your friends and lovers?
And finally, did you in fact die of a lethal cancer, or were you one of the
very first victims of AIDS, which at that time almost no one had ever
heard of?

We met when I was starting my second year at the university and
my first—in those days the courses there were at night so there was no
schedule conflict—at the School of Theater. Until then, I mean up to
the moment when your appearance shook things up and turned them
upside down (what you could not suspect and not even I knew for sure
was to what degree I was longing that something or someone—certainly someone, because for me everything comes from the hands of

someone—would turn my life upside down: perhaps one of the reasons for our disagreement, the fatal misunderstanding that arose between the two of us, was that, while you were yearning for someone to give order and stability to your life, I, a romantic and nonconformist little bourgeoise, was on the contrary yearning to have someone plant chaos in mine), my parents had not raised any objections to my plan to become an actress: in my father's case, because he was hardly aware of what was going on at home (in the fifties it was not uncommon that the home and the children be relegated to the woman's sphere, but in my father's case it was more than that, I think that although he loved us, he had given up trying to understand any of the three of us—his wife and his two children—and as for my brother, who jabbered contradictory speeches with lightning speed, he must not have understood half the words he uttered), and in my mother's, because she did not take seriously my vocation as an actress, not so much because she did not believe in my talent as because she imagined—and time would prove her right—that I would not persevere in such a difficult endeavor, or because she liked the theater and that made her more benevolent toward the profession (although it seemed to her totally unacceptable for her own daughter), or because she thought I would confine myself to amateur performances, or in the worst case go on stage—maybe for a benefit performance—to recite poetry (ever since my early childhood, as far back as I can remember, I had climbed up on chairs to recite the poems of Bécquer or the fiery verses of "La marcha triunfal"* or "El 2 de mayo," but also since early childhood, I had improvised staging and sets in the playroom or on the terrace, in summertime in the garden, to perform with other children plays almost always of my own invention) like Berta Singerman, which was less harmful and not viewed in such a bad light, not only because it did not necessarily imply a deep involvement in the world of show business, but also because according to the scale of values of my mother and the milieu she was a part of (where she was nonetheless the most liberal and permissive: a real act of defiance to believe that marriage was not the only possible profession for women, to allow me to attend the university and the School of Theater; a real act of defiance to accept the idea that my brother, a boy, take painting classes at a center where women posed in the nude, at a time when the phrase "the nude in art is not a sin" was an insincere statement divorced from reality: the nude might not be a sin in museums, but would not on your life appear on the walls of our homes), being a rhapsodist did not entail as much disrepute as being an actress, and being a pianist or a singer of lieder was still less badly regarded than being a rhapsodist (above all, and this was a determining factor, if you reached the top, because losers never aroused in my mother the least sympathy, just as criminals never aroused the least compassion: in man's hunt for his fellow man, I was always in the band of the prey, whatever might have been their crimes, and she was in the band of the hunters), although what my mother really desired, ever since we crawled around on the thick hooked rugs with a Bauhaus design while sucking our thumb (never a pacifier, which according to her was a fraud and a trick—the baby believed it was sucking in food but was only ingesting air—and in our home lies and deception were not permitted, even in the treatment of babies), was that, happily joining an artistic vocation and respectability (the money must have seemed secondary to her, because in my parents' home money was almost never discussed), I become a novelist, and my brother an architect—absurd schemes cooked up by foolish mothers!

One afternoon a friend came looking for me at the School of Theater to propose that I play the role of Helen in *La casa oscura*. I think that you, whom I did not know, had seen me perform in a university production of *All My Sons* and had liked it. Moreover, in the Arthur Miller* work I played the mother, a tragic character of about the same age as Helen—all of us at the School of Theater and in the university theater groups were too young for those roles—and although in the photographs I still have I am surprised at the clumsiness of the makeup, it did not turn out badly. I had never been offered such a fantastic role with as many dramatic possibilities as that of Helen, and I had never seen or read from any postwar author—not even Sastre or Buero,* who were working in different and opposite directions from other authors of the early Franco period—such a strong and creative work. Not a trace of *costumbrismo*,* of historical drama, of subversive or pro-regime propaganda, of the petty morals then in vogue. Pure tragedy, going directly back to Shakespeare, and beyond that, to the Greek tragedians. In that unbridled play of passions, which could unfold in any time or any place, you had not even assigned the characters Spanish names. And for the Spain of the fifties, when the big stage hits were *La herida luminosa*, *El divino impaciente* and *En Flandes se ha puesto el sol*,* it was a terribly scandalous and obscene work. Do you remember that we read some scenes on the most progressive radio station of the day—I read the monologue where Helen confesses to her son having hated him ever since she carried him in her womb—and there immediately poured in a flood of irate phone calls, many to the radio station and a few to my home, because it seems that that afternoon an infinite number of conservative housewives, and aunts and friends of my mother, were at home glued to the radio, and they could not wait to seize the phone up in arms, so that when I got home from the broadcasting station, my mother asked me (more curious than angry, maybe even secretly amused, because she could not care less about the opinion of my stuffy aunts and their hypocritical friends—some of whom left their homes to attend Mass or the Rosary, and then accidentally left their prayer book or their mantilla in the house of call, and she did not yet know—she would very soon, and then she would indeed dig up the battle-axe—that you existed and that your presence could seriously disrupt my life, our lives) what the devil had taken place that afternoon on the radio?

The fact is that that first assault on the part of respectable society filled all of us who were collaborating on the work with a militant and subversive zeal which heightened our enthusiasm and the belief that we were doing something important, while our only concern was that at any moment, maybe even before the premiere, they would cancel authorization for the performances. Indeed we could not understand how it had evaded the fierce censorship of the era, which systematically vetoed not only political and religious works that were out of step with the government or the Catholic Church, but also the slightest hint of sensuality, of unruly and thus sinful sexuality, and even the works of Lorca, Alberti, and Casona* which did not uphold subversive ideas of any kind except through the personalities of their authors. Nor would I understand why three years later they put out a deluxe edition of *La casa oscura* (not the low-cost paperback edition that was usually made for the actors' use), illustrated with drawings and photographs taken over the course of the rehearsals—the play never opened—in the Teatro Romea* (do you remember? in the freezing, empty hall, you in the stage box, more divined than seen in the shadows, your face tilted to one side with an attentive look, your eyes shining, your lips ready to break out in a smile, and I on the stage, burning, filled and intoxicated with your words, overflowing with the beauty of your words), photographs from which upon my request I had been excluded, and bound in leather, financed, you said, by the religious order to which Father

Arturo belonged, and I could not believe or understand it, because as devoted as you were in body and soul to religion, as much as you wished to put your life in order and attended Mass and received Communion every morning, as much as the dedication, if it was not obviously dedicated to the Eternal Father, was to your earthly father and not to me, who in no way wanted to put your life in order, or mine or anyone else's (the copy you gave me had the handwritten dedication: "Love can still hope, when reason despairs," which also surprised me, because for me the three years that had elapsed had relegated our story, although it had been very intense, although it had made me happy and miserable to degrees difficult to surpass, although it had perhaps marked me forever, to my prehistory, without any possibility of resurrection, and I wonder if thirty years later you also fantasized about the possibility of somehow reviving the past), and however subtle and personal and tendentious a reading Father Arturo made of the work and sold to the congregation, it would be extremely hard to view it, not only as a pious or moralistic work, but even as one of conflicting and profound metaphysical or religious concerns.

I undoubtedly fell in love, first of all, with your talent—wasn't talent the remarkable thing about you, the thing that set you apart?—I also undoubtedly fell in love with your work—is there by chance any place where we reside more intimately, more entirely than in our work? Shouldn't one seek to find every artist more in what he writes, what he paints, what he sculpts, what he composes, what he films, than in what he does or above all what he says?—but I also loved you for what you were and what you represented. As a bourgeois nonconformist of eighteen years, I was waiting for someone—a rebel, an outlaw, a deserter, no longer a Prince Charming, because my fantasies had changed upon leaving adolescence, and I was seeking an antihero rather than a hero— to blow my world—the world of my kin, where I had never felt happy or fit in, a déclassée, and who knows why, since my birth—to bits, and take me aboard his pirate ship with the black sails, or carry me off to cross the frozen steppes by his side (I Gray Wolf, with sightless eyes; you Kazan,* hybrid of dog and wolf, vulnerable only to tenderness, for someone like me, also always devoted to half-breeds), not to place me behind him on a white horse with reins of gold and carry me off with him to his palace to make me his queen. And I believed, what a colossal blunder, that it could be you: I loved in you, among so many other things, an accomplice in the rebellion, a life plan, hoping to become by your side what I deeply longed to be (I had exchanged some fantasies for others, but I was still living in Neverland,* in a world basically made of dreams) and did not feel able to become yet by myself.

How much time has passed since then, Eduardo! I had trouble with the makeup, to make myself appear many years older than I was; now I would need rejuvenating makeup, and before long my figure, my bearing, my body language would make it impossible for me to portray a middle-aged woman like Helen; then I was the youngest in all or almost all of the meetings and groups, now I find myself more and more often being the oldest, and I wonder, like almost all human beings, how it could have happened, not because life seems to me short, nor even because time, another cliché, passes more and more quickly, but because it is difficult for me to understand and accept that what at one moment was no longer is and is lost forever, and that the time gone is irretrievable, and even more irretrievable as those with whom we shared it gradually disappear (you died at the age of fifty, but your friend assured me that you looked thirty-five, and the letters from the last stage of your life are as lively, as fresh, as passionate, as ingenuous as those you wrote me in the fullness of youth, and in them you reproach me for my sparks of cynicism, my skeptical attitude, my wells of bitterness, in them you reproach me simply because I *have* grown old). So much time has passed, Eduardo, that the memories I have kept alive, that I need only close my eyes to recover, are by now very few.

I remember, as I said before, the rehearsals in the Teatro Romea, the wait in the foyer until Marsillach* came out, who was rehearsing with his troupe just before us, and then the wide, dark and empty space of the theater, the cold, which I did not feel, your form on the proscenium (I have just discovered that to recall your face I am resorting more to photographs than to the memory I hold in my mind), and running between the two of us the prodigious thread—never broken, because neither you nor the director ever burst into my long monologues with a suggestion or a comment—the extremely sensual and heartrending thread of your words, words that I took from you and then returned to you revitalized, reborn in my voice, in a strange and morbid ceremony of communion or of procreation, which is among the most erotic memories of my life. I remember that some days at noon, upon finishing the rehearsal, we would all go to eat something at the corner bar, but other times they left us alone, and we descended the Ramblas*—hand in hand and as though on wings—to the sea, and the middle finger of the hand holding mine separated from the others for a moment and scratched me, tickling my palm, and my heart beat faster, because that was love and no more explicit caress would make me quiver with the exact same intensity, and then you abruptly stopped, you took me by the shoulders, turned me toward you, looked me in the eyes—your eyes were laughing, and my eyes were laughing, because not all was anguish and fear, not all was interminable confessions of anxiety and sorrow, but there were also in our story moments of euphoria, of abandonment, of happiness, you perhaps better equipped than anyone for joy—and you said "hello," and that "hello" seemed to me the sweetest expression of love that in my eighteen years I had ever heard; warmer and more tender the memory of your finger on my palm, your hands on my shoulders, your eyes on mine, than that of those kisses, too greedy and voracious, those touches and caresses, too eager and insistent, too frustrating—at least for me, who have always hated secrecy—of our later dates at the most remote tables of some sordid spots in the low part of the city, when my mother had dug up the battle-axe and I had begun, for the first time in my life, to lie like mad: about where I was, about whom I was with, about what I was doing, and I had inevitably—and this made them more awkward—involved others in my lies, because from the moment my mother put on the war paints and alerted my father, I was only allowed to see you during rehearsals—they had not yet dared to forbid me from acting in the production—and all other meetings and letters and phone calls were culpable or at least clandestine. I also remember that, a few days after we met, the whole company had arranged to attend a concert together at the Palau,* and by an unexpected coincidence, no one else showed up, so the two of us were alone in two seats on the top floor, and I was so agitated, my heart was beating so hard in my chest, that I was afraid the entire theater would discover us and the orchestra would miss a beat, and all the spectators would turn around to look at us accusingly with pointed finger, and we both made a conscious effort, took exquisite care not to touch each other, stiff in our seats like two dummies, hands in our laps, scarcely leaning our elbows on the armrests, as though any contact would be not only compromising but dangerous, as though we sensed that the slightest involuntary brush could unleash a cataclysm, that the building might burn down—why not, if even at a distance sparks flew from your skin to my skin?—or the ride of the stone Valkyries run over us, or the roof above our heads or the floor beneath our feet give way.

My mother had dug up the battle-axe, she had alerted my father—
usually so oblivious to whatever was going on at home, to what his children were or were not doing—to what was happening or what could
shortly happen; she also for the first time in my life monitored my
comings and goings and my class hours; she called the homes of my
girlfriends where I had said or she had deduced that I would be; she
snooped around and examined me upon my return (and I could not
help blushing to the roots of my hair, afraid she would spot the traces of
your kisses on my swollen lips, of your teeth on my neck, of reeking of
the smoke and cheap wine from the filthy bars you took me to for our
furtive encounters), and it is even possible—she has never told me and
I have never asked: in fact we never again spoke of you or *La casa oscura*
when it was all over—that she had me followed by a detective who gave
a detailed account of my adventures—in actuality so innocent—and,
what could have been more dangerous and compromising, of your adventures when you were not with me. I do not know if, assuming he did
exist, he included in the report of my daily activities the strange visits to
a monastery, because at that time, willing to resort to any means that
could help us get ahead, I had gotten in touch with Father Arturo—a
young friar, slender, handsome, undoubtedly brilliant—and we had entered into a holy alliance with the aim of achieving your salvation: we
both wished you well, but I wanted you egoistically for myself and he
supposedly wanted you first and foremost for God.

I will never know—it is one of the missing pieces in the puzzle and
they will not let me fill it in—what he felt for you, I will never know if
his rashness in involving me—I was after all a youngster of eighteen
who had learned everything from books, and you were what you were,
and that "what you were" could not disturb me, in fact it did not disturb me, but I think it must have scandalized or upset him—in his apostolic plans, in encouraging me not to break off with you but to remain
by your side, was due to an overwhelming innocence, an improbable
candor—didn't he sometimes send you to stay with his own family in
the town? didn't he allow or promote a close friendship between you
and his younger brother, who was little more than an adolescent, who
appeared in photographs with one of your arms around his shoulders
or waist, wearing swapped articles of clothing?—or due to a more-or-
less conscious passion, in any case one that was intense enough to make
him, clad in apostolic zeal and taking the name of God in vain, lose the
most elemental sense of discretion and run over everything. (Don't

worry, Eduardo, I do not despise him at all, nor does it occur to me to add him to the long list of priests and brethren who, according to what you read in novels and hear from friends, laid their hands on defenseless students.)

What is certain is that he and I began meeting alone in the visitors' lounge, an immense room with chairs lining the four walls, and we had long and secret discussions—not completely secret, since you heard doctored up versions of some of them—concerning your earthly and eternal salvation (the former, which was of greater interest to me, should inevitably lead to the latter), about what was the best course for you to take (there was complete agreement on the idea that you should leave the home of your father and stepmother, finish your university degree, find paid work, and above all, break off your relationship with the shopkeeper), about what I should or should not do, the role I should adopt and play for your good; we played at being Daddy and Mommy, a Daddy and Mommy to whose lot had fallen a marvelous but difficult little one, whom one should without letup (with affection, with tenderness, but with firmness, and always counting on the aid of the Almighty, who also took a very special and particular interest in you— oh, the fascination of the prodigal son and the stray sheep!—whom the three of us turned to in our prayers) guide and lead. If the detective— assuming there was a detective and he had followed me to the monastery—had installed hidden microphones in the visiting room and had given a full account to my parents of what was discussed there, I think that their fury (they would not have believed for a moment in the candor of Father Arturo, they who did not even believe in God, nor felt, although they were right-wing, great sympathy for the clergy) would have reached high places and caused heads to roll.

But it was not necessary for them to have a complete account of my monastic discussions for the bomb to go off that had long been buried, as I was well aware, beneath my feet. My parents summoned me, with grave expressions, to the library—the room of the house where important matters were discussed and big tellings-off were given, also where we occasionally rehearsed when there was no theater available—they sat me down before them and informed me—my mother more pleased, Papa more contrite—that their suspicions and fears had not only been confirmed but exceeded all their expectations, that you had been arrested several times in bars of ill repute, all-male bars, and that there was a file listing you as a homosexual at the Central Police Headquarters. And I was left speechless, but not with surprise. I was speechless because there was nothing I could tell them that they would understand, although it was the simple truth: that I already knew or intuited or suspected it (you yourself had given me clues pointing in that direction, although you had never said it openly, maybe because you were waiting for me to ask and I never did), and that, aside from the consequences it could have, it did not matter to me too much: that for some reason impossible to explain, impossible even then to explain to myself, your relations with other boys—in contrast to your more-or-less venal relationship with the shopkeeper, object of both Father Arturo's and my burning hatred—did not arouse in me rejection or repugnance or, what was more surprising, even jealousy. I could not tell my parents that never, since I first heard of their existence, and despite the fact that in the Spain of the fifties not only were they considered to be criminal but were painted in the most repulsive and somber colors, did such relations seem to me abominable (it is also true that at that stage, in the second year at the university and the first in the School of Theater, we had all secretly read Lorca and Proust and Genet, and *The Fruits of the Earth** had opened before me bright tempting paths until then forbidden), despite the fact that up until then I had never felt any inclination toward another woman (unless we include my feelings, so ardent but so angelic, first for my mother and then for Berta Singerman), I had never been shocked by the relations of men with other men, of women with other women.

So when I heard what they were telling me—my mother more pleased ("We told you so"), Papa more sorry ("You'll get over it, you'll see, although you don't think so now, you'll get over it")—I realized that there was no possible line of argument, no room for an agreement or compromise or deal, nothing to negotiate, and I immediately decided to throw over Father Arturo, our prayers and our communions, the hope in the Lord's partiality for prodigal sons and stray sheep, in the help afforded by communing with the saints and, on the other hand, by your desire for safety and stability, since the only thing that would have been worth negotiating about and trying to save from the wreckage—your work and my part in it—had finally gone down the drain: now they would not allow me at any price to go ahead with the rehearsals. So I did not try to defend you, to defend us, which I knew to be futile, and I bit my tongue and prudently refrained from saying that it seemed to me disgraceful that homosexuality was a crime in the eyes of the law, and even more disgraceful that indiscriminate people were rounded up in collective police raids simply because they happened to be on particular premises, and more disgraceful still that for that reason they opened a criminal file on them, that remained forever in the police records, not to mention the fact that such files, which should at least have been extremely confidential, were accessible to and at the disposal of law-abiding people, respectable people like my own parents, bourgeois families who had the sacred right to protect their little ones from the perverts, perverts who, in your case, belonged to a much lower social class, which made them infinitely more vulnerable (if you had displayed one of the resounding names of the upper-crust families of the city, I doubt you would have spent even a few hours at the police station—they had detained you, it seems, for several nights, and just thinking about it made me sick with distress—or that they would have opened on you any file whatsoever, and there is no doubt that if they had, it would not have been eternal or accessible to anyone).

So I decided then, in a matter of seconds, that the time had come to break with everything, to forget God—who knew if He was even on our side—and Father Arturo and our catechistic meetings, to bestride the rump of your black horse, to board your pirate ship with its outlaw crew, to traverse by your side (I Gray Wolf, a blind female; you Kazan, potent crossbreed of dog and wolf) the frozen steppes of Alaska, loin against loin, defending with savage thrusts our survival and our love and our happiness. And when I met you at our usual café (an elegant tearoom on the Paseo de Gracia,* where we had sat alone together for the first time just a few months before, surrounded by well-bred women sipping tea and gorging themselves on pastries, lowering our voices—I have just noticed that I cannot recall the sound of your voice, I remember your eyes, unusually almond-shaped and dark, which gave you a certain Oriental look so at the university you were sometimes known as the Egyptian, I remember your fine and well-etched eyebrows, your smooth, soft, slightly rosy complexion, but I do not recall your voice, or the smell of your skin, or the taste of your mouth, or the touch of your hands, or your particular way of walking and smiling, so I remember hardly anything!—so that amid the henlike din in which they exchanged trivialities they would not pick up our words, so unsuitable we thought for their ears, without our hands even brushing but with our hearts beating fast, a café where we later met many times at hours when it was half empty, and which alternated with the dives of the Ramblas where you kissed me until my neck and lips were black and blue, you squeezed me until leaving me breathless, you got me drunk on words and caresses), so when I met you at our usual café, for a last meeting authorized by my parents, to inform you, they thought, that we would never see each other again, I had the firm intention to run away with you, I had drawn up a detailed plan (my greatest lunacies and even my worst stupidities have always been carefully programmed in advance). By a miracle (especially in your case, and in the fifties) we both had passports in order, I had enough money so I would not even be obliged to steal some (which circumstance would not have stopped me or mattered to me too much), and before anyone would suspect that I was not, as was assumed, spending the weekend at the home of a girlfriend, we would have crossed two borders and reached our destination, which would be an Italian city—we both liked Italy—and why not Milan, big enough so it would be feasible to disappear there and which also happened to be the name—and this could be premonitory or at least a happy coincidence—of the tearoom where we met many mornings? Once there we would think up some way to survive—I stubbornly insistent, as I have always been, that money is not an insurmountable problem and ends up turning up somewhere; you then convinced that it is the crux of almost all problems—and although it was inevitable that sooner or later they would find us, so much time would have passed by then that there would be little they could do (I was sure that they would force us to marry, and I imagine you were sure, and maybe you were not far wrong, that they would put me into a Swiss convent, and have you jailed for running off with a minor).

I, a spoiled and imaginative girl who had learned everything from movies and books, given to romanticism and with a marked tendency toward melodrama, sure of winning, bet for all or nothing: either run off together or never see each other again. And yet I did not confess to you, I did not even insinuate the reason for my parents' irrevocable decision, which had left me without counterarguments, and of course I refused to let you go to talk with them, as you proposed, but I did not tell you why my father, so civilized, so understanding, so tolerant, was capable of throwing you down the stairs if you showed your good intentions and asked for my hand (the fact that Mama would scratch your eyes out with her nails was less significant), and I wonder if he would even have been capable of denouncing you to the police, that police who were kind enough to open for them their records. You, for your part, did not take seriously my parents' decision or my ultimatum, convinced that, if not right away, after some days, at most a few weeks, we would meet again in secret, that everything would remain the same, that with time even my parents might finally relent. And yet, Eduardo (and I realize now, I realized a long time ago, that I was unjust: you were not the Barbary Pirate, or Sandokan, or the Flying Dutchman,* or the hybrid of dog and wolf that crossed, Gray Wolf tight by your side, the Alaskan steppes, you were just an insecure, troubled boy, seeking tenderness and safety—maybe even respectability—who longed, and I could not understand this, to enter the orderly world—dirty but orderly—of respectable people, of my elders, which I in contrast sought to escape from: you were a poor boy who bore on his fragile shoulders a great talent, disproportionate to his scant strength and which he finally would not know what to do with), and yet, Eduardo, that morning, without your suspecting it, was the beginning of the end of our story.

However, you were right about one thing. After some time had passed, and not even so much time, after a few days, shut up in my room and not going out—what was the point of going out if I was not going to meet you?—not answering the telephone for anyone—why answer the phone if it could not be you?—not being able to focus my attention on the pages of a book or on anything, eating hardly at all and not attending to anything I was told (Mama: "We told you so"; Papa: "Everything passes; this too will pass"), not doing anything but sob with my face buried in the pillow or turned stubbornly toward the wall (my parents believed, and have always gone on believing—not even Mama, so suspicious, so vindictive and half psychic, could on that occasion suspect what was for her an unthinkable truth: for once my foolishness had exceeded all her suspicions—for having fallen in love with an unsuitable person, a bad guy, when I was only crying because you had not loved me enough, because you had not had enough guts to run away with me), some normalcy was restored. I had my debut, as had been planned, coinciding with the performances given by the Bayreuth company* in Barcelona: the Teatro Liceo* our temple, the temple of a provincial and spineless bourgeoisie; Wagner our high priest or our lesser god. A long dress of deep blue tulle, which I had not even tried on, a white fox-fur stole, which I had not seen or chosen, silver high-heeled sandals, which I could not walk on with the slightest ease, the cultured-pearl necklace they had given me upon graduating from high school: the complete getup of a true-blue upper-middle-class girl, although it seemed a bit strange that I spent part of the performance crying—identifying with the distress, humiliation and abandonment of the Valkyrie, and holding you responsible for the betrayal, no less blameworthy for being involuntary, of Siegfried,* and although, to properly remain in mourning for you, or because my friends of that time, almost all literature or theater students, did not go well with this type of celebration, there was no party. I also returned to the university, just in time to take, without getting very brilliant grades but without failing, the final exams for the year. So I began again to go out, to talk to people, to get on the phone, to concentrate on a book or a movie, to eat normally and even, although I would not have admitted it, to have moments when I did not think about you, when I felt happy and was able to laugh.

And then, one fine day upon leaving the School of Theater, there you were by the door to the garden, a little abashed and scared, with your tenderest look and your most seductive smile, more than ever a babe lost in the woods, at the mercy of wild beasts and evil witches. And you embraced me tightly and kissed me on the lips (a bold gesture, not because we were in front of many of my classmates, who would not have blanched at that or a lot more, but because in those early years of the Caudillo, it was a crime to kiss in the street or even in a doorway or inside a car) and whispered sweet words in my ear, how much you had missed me, how hard it had been to respect for so many days my desire not to see each other, how much you realized that you loved me. And I, despite all my resolutions not to and all my doubts (what would the Valkyrie have done, would she have been capable of resisting if Siegfried had sworn that it had all been a mistake for which the gods were to blame, that he had loved her alone?), let you go ahead. And after that we saw each other four or five times in secret—if my parents found out about these meetings, they never alluded to them—again occupying the most remote and darkest tables of some shady bars, which seemed to me ever less romantic and ever more seedy.

And then came the summer and we separated, and you wrote me regularly beautiful love letters, which I awaited with excitement, read with pleasure, and sometimes answered. However, I was now by what would be the same sea as all my summers, in an old convent situated in the mountains, where female university students of the time went through the obligatory social service program, a hostel of the Falange, which I went to against my will but because I knew that sooner or later I would have to go through it (otherwise they would not give you a degree or a passport), but it turned out to be a beautiful place, and every afternoon I ran up the hill to the town where your letters arrived and every morning I ran down the other hill leading to the sea, and I swam with pleasure until I was exhausted, worn out and happy, and I found it stimulating living in close proximity, until then an unknown experience for me, with other girls my age, all university students but from different colleges, and I enthusiastically took part not only in theatrical readings and poetry recitals and campfires and political discussions, but even in early morning activities and gymnastics and choir, activities I knew I was congenitally hopeless in, and I spent entire nights debating and conversing—in a packed dark cell, in low voices, so they would not find us out—with my companions until dawn—so spectacular the sunrise on the horizon of the sea—and I made friendships that would continue afterwards, and I met Mercedes, whom I would love until death and beyond death, the first of the two people (there would be only two, she and later Esteban) who would bring me to accept myself fully as I was and to be reconciled with the world, filling in gaps and needs left by my mother, and through Mercedes, the intelligent, inflammatory and heterodox speeches she substituted for what should have been "classes to form the national spirit," for the first time I got interested in politics, I became a little more aware that the world did not come down to falling in love and getting on a stage or writing poems, that it was a place full of injustice and sorrow, which I could not remain apart from and which I was to some degree responsible for, and I had arrived at this belated revelation by unwonted paths (Falange classes in a hostel of the Sección Femenina),* but I had arrived there nonetheless. And then my parents, tired of my causing them problems, banished me to Madrid, to get me away from the theater and separate me from you, and I had the experience of living a whole year away from home in a strange city, among people with backgrounds and attitudes different from my own, a city moreover full of theaters and museums, but without the sea. And although we continued exchanging beautiful love letters (mine ever less sincerely felt and more literary), and although we saw each other when I returned home for the Christmas and Easter vacations, by then you had stopped being—without my intending this, certainly without my wishing it—the center of my life.

Many years later (in fact it must not have been more than four or five, but at that time so many things were happening, so many discoveries and changes took place in a year, that time seemed to expand to make room for them so all perspectives on the past are hopelessly distorted), I would receive a letter from you written in the Novitiate of San Estanislao, Cochabamba, Bolivia, in which you refer to one from me, which I do not recall having written and which had come into your hands after going all around the world and with two years' delay, and in which apparently I, unaware that you were on the other side of the ocean, invited you to meet me at Milán, our usual café. "What can I write to you?" you say. "What should I write, given that I am now a friar? A formal letter? No, to you never. I will speak to you as always, and if possible with greater sincerity. As though I had really kept your date on the Day of the Epiphany.* The only thing I will do, if you allow me, is to change the time of meeting. Milán is much cozier in the morning, when the chairs are still upside down and there is only room in the sections on the left. So it is nine o'clock on a winter morning and this time I have enough money to invite you for a cup of coffee . . . ," and it is not a bad beginning, but then you go on: "I have so many things to tell you. For the most part, crazy schemes. You know what I am like. But there is one that takes my breath away: to be a priest of Christ. Why? Probably because someone, a long time ago, asked God for the best for me. And God heard that prayer . . . We cannot complain that God—the God whom you taught me to love—has granted me what you one day asked Him for without knowing what you were asking." And further on: "You and Arturo put your own peace at risk to help me. But without your help Arturo would have failed, because at that time I was not willing to accept aid that was offered to me only in the name of Christ . . . You saved me, because by your side I could easily renounce the demonic and suicidal desire to endow life at any cost with the greatest degree of intensity." And then: "You were for me the mother I had lost, the sister I never had, the best friend, the lover every adolescent dreams of . . . You were the promise of a perfect wife."

I never answered that letter (I do not even remember if I had waited for you a long time years before at Milán, if I was very disappointed that you did not show up, and how typical of me to blindly summon you, at a time when we had obviously stopped seeing each other, to that date on the Day of the Epiphany, as a gift perhaps of the Magi!), because I was absorbed in other endeavors, sunk in other obsessions, and your form was fading into a remote past (much more distant—I said that temporal perspectives are capricious—than I feel you to be now), or because it seemed to me simply a bit of nonsense, in which it was difficult for me to recognize you or recognize myself, and to which I had nothing to add or object. It was only upon learning that you had died, that I was never going to see you again and there would not be a coming to terms between the two of us, that I searched for it among old papers—a heap of letters with the ink now faded, a picture of you with Arturo's brother and a little girl in your arms, another in the Romea, another on the beach of Santander,* none in which we appeared together, and a spiral-bound school notebook with squared paper where I had copied in my best hand one of your works, which I do not know if it survives elsewhere, *Diálogos en la penumbra**—and I found it and reread it with care. It is a strange letter. Not the letter itself, which is transparent, coherent, linear, almost out of a stylebook, to a degree that I wonder if you did not end up writing the formal letter you had intended to avoid, but rather you (or the image that I had forged and retained of you) wrote it to me (or the image that I kept of myself).

At some point there must have been a misunderstanding, one more disconnect in a story plagued with multiple and repeated disconnects, because at no point did it occur to me that, if I was asking God for the best for you—as I surely must have done, since at that time, despite having read from cover to cover Sartre and Beauvoir* and even Voltaire, and having made *The Fruits of the Earth* into my bedside reading, I still believed in a personal God who, along with maintaining the difficult equilibrium of the universe and orchestrating the music of the spheres, took a personal interest in our problems and with whom one could converse respectfully but on familiar terms at any hour of the day or night—that that "best" could refer to a plan in which we would not be together, which would leave me out (it did not matter so much if it also included others, but it could not exclude me), and it did not even cross my mind that your future could consist in being ordained a priest on the other side of the world, in a place I would not have been able to locate on a map. I am afraid that I never even took your religiousness very seriously: strange and unjust as it might have been, I think that I never took it as seriously as I took my own, at times—only at times and not for very long—mystical and ecstatic. And never ever—despite playing at Daddy and Mommy with Father Arturo—did I fantasize about being your mother, or your sister, or your friend in body or soul, and never ever, not for you nor for anyone, have I been the promise, much less the realization, not only of a perfect wife, but even of a halfway acceptable wife. On the other hand, I would indeed have liked to be your lover, although I do not know if I would have been the type of lover every adolescent dreams of. In any case, you would always, until the hour of your death, for better or for worse, be a child, and I will probably be an adolescent until the hour of mine, and between a child and an adolescent there can be imaginative and sumptuous and varying forms of perversion, but nothing resembling the stable and moderately happy marriage between two adults. But above all, Eduardo, I did not try nor at any moment would have tried to dissuade you from the desire, as demonic and suicidal as it might be, to attain in life at any cost the highest degree of intensity, because paradoxically and apparently without your suspecting it, that desire was almost the only thing we had in common. And I say "almost" because at that time there was something more: the blind and devout faith in your talent.

Not in that letter nor in those you wrote me ages later from Buenos Aires do you say a word about your work (nor would your Argentine friend in our one and only interview, because I could have been drugged, asleep or half a zombie, but I swear I would have been aware of that), nor did I ask you about it in mine (overcome by the same reserve, the same respect, that had prevented me from alluding even to your relations with other men, one's writing being more intimate than one's lovers), and this was surely the most important thing that in our interview, frustrated by your death, ill timed in so many respects and thus the last of our disconnects, I could have ascertained, the key piece in the hard-to-assemble puzzle of your life. Where, Eduardo, are the works you should have written, the works you were born to write, that should have been as essential to you, as inevitable as the air you breathed? What did you do with that heap of ideas and projects, with your prodigious gift for creating characters and dramatic situations, for combining words? Has it all come down to a work in one act published in an exquisite and absurd edition, read in a university summer course (and I did not even play the role of Helen) and, as far as I know, never produced? To another unfinished work, copied by me by hand in a school notebook, kept in the drawer of my nostalgias, and about which I am not even sure if there exists another copy or if anyone else knows of it? To helping an old actress and rhapsodist write her memoirs? I simply cannot understand it; I am not capable of imagining how such a blunder could have occurred. Because whatever you did or did not do over the course of your life, whatever you were proud of or ashamed of or felt guilty about, your marvelous or sordid, or marvelous and sordid stories of love and friendship, your little dirty tricks and shady deals, your tender or terrible gestures, your lies and your truths, your fits of childish egoism or of endearing generosity, all the bad and all the good that you did or that was done to you are without importance, but the fact that you wasted your talent does not deserve forgiveness, either from God or from men, and it is something that neither will I forgive.

Eduardo, dearest, so tender, handsome, seductive, imaginative, endearing, my unforgettable love, I greatly fear that, if by chance you were right and I am wrong, if there really does exist, against all odds, a Supreme Being who takes a personal interest in us, boring insects relegated to the most remote corner of the most wretched of galaxies, who loves us each and every one and follows the course of our lives, and if this Supreme Being has given in to the curious whim of judging us at the hour of our death, I greatly fear, my poor love, that when I arrive there, I will find you seated like an Egyptian scribe before the gates of the Kingdom of Heaven, in the white oversleeves of a scribbler, applying yourself diligently to capturing on paper with an angel's plumes* the works you should have written and did not write here below.

Letter to Esteban
(at last the Flying Dutchman)

You MADE YOUR DEFINITIVE RETURN TO ITHACA* IN THE EARLY SIXTIES, after fifteen years of exile during which you just appeared in August to spend the month of vacation with your children, fifteen years in which you had not gone through the rigors of a single winter, so there you were in mid-November, having recently fled your home and numb with the cold—in this city of mine where the climate is supposed to be invariably mild and heating is reserved, or in those days was reserved, for almost luxury housing—shut up in the well-furnished but freezing room you had rented from an elderly couple of good birth but unable to get by on the husband's retirement pension, typing for hours and hours on the typewriter, almost all those that were not taken by your job as a sales representative to bookstores for a catalog of art books, a job you had gotten at once from a newspaper ad and that, given your age, which at that time seemed to me advanced, because you were about to turn or had just turned forty, and given the affluent life of a business executive that you had led in the Americas, seemed to me heroic, but that you did not once complain about, because the fact is that at that time you did not complain about anything, and it was surprising to me that, with your double work as a traveling salesman and a home translator, you were always free to see me at the exact moment I proposed getting together. You translated from English—which you had learned as a young man from an English girlfriend—beneath the blanket which one of your women writer friends had given you upon your leaving home and knowing you were cold, a woman you had met nonetheless through your wife who, Lord knows why, frequented the artistic and intellectual world composed of painters, filmmakers, photographers, models, architects, writers and publishers, the prehistory of what would soon become a *gauche divine** that you would hate for its

94

frivolousness, which gathered at suppertime at the large table we had reserved in the back of the restaurant La Mariona and ended up at Jamboree,* to drink, listen to jazz, discuss everything under the sun, especially politics, and make out; so a blanket covering your knees—those thin bony knees, unmistakable, that I would love so much, as I would love every bend, every centimeter, of your angular and so soft body—and wearing some warm clothes that you had to buy urgently on a tight budget, and that, although not expensive, were becoming, because whatever you wore, you had the air of a real gentleman—it was a delight to enter shops and restaurants on your arm—whereas I, even when I have occasionally bought myself lavish clothes, never shed a certain ragamuffin look.

You returned to Ithaca and, of course, you had not conquered Troy (on the other hand, at that time you would have preferred Paris and Helen to Menelaus*—purely out of loyalty to your own would you perhaps have aligned yourself reluctantly on the Greek side), but you had earned—as had other friends of yours who had also emigrated to the Americas and returned with enough capital to lead a more than comfortable life, to devote themselves to writing their books or directing their films—quite a lot of money, of which soon after your arrival and within days of meeting me, you would discover that none remained, and it was very typical of you, who never learned how or was willing to negotiate defeats, to leave Venezuela on a sudden impulse and leave everything in the hands of your partner and friend, who would write you a very long, detailed letter in which he assured you that he could not salvage anything, either from your part of the business or from your personal belongings, including your car, he had almost suffered losses himself making off with everything you owned, and to my amazement as a middle-class girl, used to the idea that when friends of my parents were ruined and declared themselves bankrupt, and closed down the textile mills, the chains of stores or restaurants—which gave rise to an inconsiderate and unjustified anger on the part of the workers and employees who found themselves out on the street—they still had properties somewhere in the Maresme or the Vallès,* a fantastic apartment or villa in Barcelona, in the wife's name, a second home on the coast or in the Pyrenees, also in the wife's name (yes, as a child I firmly believed that the Civil War was started by the Reds—I had never heard of Republicans—and I also believed that, for some reason that was beyond my grasp, the real estate always had to be in the name of the wife), and an absurd wad of forgotten stock shares in a corner of the safe (accounts in Switzerland were rarely spoken of and in low voices), to my surprise, then, in your case there was no vestige of past splendor to resort to in hard times. Not only no foreign bank accounts (it would have been extremely easy to open an account in dollars in New York, because you were dealing with North American firms), or property—the apartments were rented—but not even jewelry, fur coats—your Penelope did not work, but she did not have bourgeois whims or fancies— art works, an important library, a stamp collection or a good watch: when it came to not having things, you did not even have a coat. You had earned quite a lot of money engaged in activities that did not interest you, had squandered it with largesse, had distributed it generously, and in the meantime had lived out love stories with many colorful women, always, like those of Ulysses,* and on occasion with the same treachery, abandoned.

It was your wife who reported all this, the legitimate one—you had not abandoned her, but you had interposed an ocean between the two of you—to whoever was interested at the table of La Mariona or Jamboree, and that image, no doubt exaggerated and literary, that she offered of her absent husband (she accused you of not failing to sleep with any girl of any race or color, from the haughtiest princess to the fisherman's daughter, who forestalled you and threw herself into your arms—because of course they were initially and principally to blame, and well deserved the subsequent abandonment—but at the same time she described you as a bold adventurer, dangerously involved in politics, a true knight errant, idealistic, honest and generous to the core) I do not think could predispose anyone against you. Many of the people there knew and respected you, they thought you were nice or had benefited from your generosity, and they listened to your wife's harangue with a condescending or amused smile, and as for me, who had never met you, you had me halfway seduced in advance. Didn't Inés fall in love with Don Juan from some letters and Brígida's* description of him? Wasn't Senta* in love with the Flying Dutchman long before he arrived at her port, moved by the legend that enveloped him? Although, of course, I was not so innocent or childlike.

I learned from her (you rarely talked about yourself unless I put you through a rigorous interrogation, impelled by the extreme need to know your past, to encompass in my love every moment of your life prior to me, whereas you did not show a particular interest in discovering mine, and were much better equipped to live fully in the present, without making it conditional on nostalgia for the past or weighing it down with fears or dreams projected into the future) that, while doing your military service, you had collaborated as a spy over the course of the Second World War, crossing the Pyrenees repeatedly, alone and on foot, to transmit to the Allies information that was given to you here—in the belief, shared by many, that if they won the contest, it would mean the immediate fall of Franco, one of so many thwarted hopes, one of so many betrayed dreams—and when they discovered the conspiracy you were a part of, by a miracle they did not sentence you to death, maybe because many fat cats would have been compromised, maybe because it was already clear that Germany was plunging inexorably toward defeat, so they never delivered a verdict, which in your case would have been summary, nor did they simply put a bullet through your head, but they confined you in the prison of Montjuic,* where you would spend almost two years. And the worst of it was—this you told me, not your wife—that from time to time they would order you to gather up all your things, they said they were going to release you, they put you through the formalities for the release from prison, and just upon crossing the threshold and taking a couple of steps, the police who were waiting there intercepted you to arrest you again and return you to your cell, such an agonizing cat-and-mouse game that, when that infernal circle was interrupted, perhaps temporarily, perhaps forever, impossible for you to know which, and you were granted a reprieve, you cleared out just like that, determined to forge a life for yourself wherever and however it might be, but far from Francoist Spain.

In this way politics repeatedly diverted you from what I think should have been your destiny, not only because any plan to enter the university evaporated—your secondary studies already interrupted for three years by the Civil War—but also because, upon leaving Montjuic, your hasty marriage was not to the English girlfriend, who in the meantime had married someone else, but to the woman whom I met, who had apparently been very good to you, visiting you often, boosting your morale, taking you food and cigarettes, and because the long period in exile would drive you into commercial activities that were very lucrative but completely foreign to your interests. And even when, so many years later, you finally decided to return to Ithaca, it was undoubtedly because you felt nostalgia for your homeland and were fed up with living abroad—almost all the Spanish friends you had met there would likewise return around that time—because you wanted to be closer to your children—who adored you then, and would adore you, I believe, until your death, as would those you had with me—but the haste and urgency of your return were also due to the fact that the conservative party there, which you had actively and openly fought against, won the election, and you must have been tired—at least temporarily—of enlisting time and again in the camp that lost every battle.

However, more than these facts, which I heard first from your wife and then from you, and which were confirmed and amplified by new information from your friends, I was moved by a story you told me that no one else could have told, because your parents had already died and I could not get in touch with your siblings: how, at the age of ten—a tall, lanky lad, as blond and as handsome as our son would be, perhaps a bit reserved and serious for his age—you cut up some confetti on April 14, 1931,* wrote on it in your best handwriting "Long live the Republic! Long live Catalonia!" and threw it onto the street from your balcony, as you said to yourself, in some distress, that everything had already been achieved and there was no pending cause for you to collaborate in: they had made the revolution without your help.

You must have returned to Barcelona at the end of July, and there were two initial fleeting, chance encounters, so fleeting that you were perhaps unaware of the first, while I was ignorant of the second until you told me about it some time later. On the first occasion you were walking down the street with your wife and some friends—it greatly irritated you that, having just arrived, instead of staying home with the children, you were dragged out night after night with a group of people some of whom you liked, but others of whom seemed to you snobbish and smug, and I wonder if years later, when things started to go wrong between the two of us, I might have paid the price for that irritation— and we said hello on passing, and given that I knew everyone except one person, I deduced that that one must be you, that strange mixture of Don Juan, the Flying Dutchman and Che Guevara* that I had fantasized about and was burning with desire to meet. You were still golden brown from the sun of the tropical beaches—bronze, not tanned—and you looked extremely handsome (when my mother met you later, she dotted the i's and crossed the t's, telling me how could you be extremely handsome with that nose, but yes, you were very attractive), it was not the least surprising that every damsel, from the haughty princess to the

peasant girl in her shabby rowboat, by way of Aminta, Tisbea, Doña
Inés, Calypso, Circe and Nausicaa, swooned in your arms and fought
intrepidly to keep you or like Dido* hurled herself into the flames upon
seeing your ship depart. And I noticed, as you were moving off, your
particular way of walking, which our children have inherited and which
allows me, ever more blind and absentminded, to recognize them at a
distance, long before distinguishing their facial features or their silhouettes: at the moment you lift your foot there's a slight upward thrust, as
though, full of optimism, you were trying to take flight, an attempt that
ends upon depositing that foot on the ground, to immediately recom-
mence with the other, so your walk consists of a continual to-and-fro
movement up and down—if you are with other people, walking in a
crowd, your heads emerge from and sink into the crowd—which lends
it a special liveliness and grace.

Then, a few days—a few nights, because at that time everything
happened at night, nocturnal vermin who abandoned our lairs at nightfall to regain them with the dawn—later, I entered a bar on the shore—
also in a pack—with my husband and with Sappho, my dachshund
puppy, in my arms, and according to what you later told me, I had such
a pathetic, helpless look—you were observing me from a table at the
back of the premises and I did not see you—I looked so emaciated and
pale—worse than pale, you insisted, azure—at a point in the summer
when everyone in the world was walking around tanned—if not golden
brown like you—by the sun, that it suddenly occurred to you that
somebody had to do something for me, and do it fast, and that that
someone might well be you (you were always moved and perhaps
aroused by the image of women who were unhappy and, you imagined,
badly loved, you were always ready to make them a sandwich, serve
them a drink, and offer them a warm refuge to cry on your shoulder,
and I wonder how you managed later, without being cruel, to abandon
them).

It's true that in those days I must have felt unhappy, tending as I did,
then much more than now, toward grand gestures and melodramatic
attitudes, with the collapse of a marriage that had lasted scarcely a year
and that had begun going under two or three months after a precipi-
tous, rather absurd wedding. But now, more than half a lifetime later, I
see no reason why anyone (much less I myself) should have pitied me. I
had gotten into that adventure of my own accord, without anyone's
pushing or encouraging me, content and in love—it's clear that I was at

certain moments and for some time in love—but frivolously and without knowing how long it would last: certainly not forever, not until death did us part. If this were not the case, why did I drag my future husband—who, it's fair to say, let himself be dragged without putting up too much resistance—six days before the wedding, to the office of an astute progressive lawyer, to devise a legal scheme—two twin letters, dated on the day of the wedding ceremony and authenticated before a notary, in which we informed each other of the decision not to have children, one of which, if need be, would be presented before the Church tribunal, while the other would be destroyed—which would allow us, in a Spain where civil marriage had just been established but divorce was still impossible, to seek an annulment? And above all, how does one tally so much caution, this plunging headfirst into the whirlpool, but knowing how to swim and putting your clothes away for safekeeping, with what was supposed to be head-over-heels love, the great love of the romantics? (At that time I again had the premonition that I was not endowed with either the virtues or the vices needed to live as a couple, and I had the vague fear, which would temporarily vanish upon falling in love with you, that I was indeed made for love, but not for the kind of love that lasts until death.) So our marriage was reduced to the childish adventure of two spoiled children (that is why it was so overwhelming, upon meeting you, to find myself before a real man, capable of making genuine commitments and carrying them through to their ultimate consequences, of assuming risks and responsibilities, who had no interest in games or frivolities), and the breakup was not traumatic or, above all, sordid; it did not leave in me, and I think neither in him, persistent marks or wounds or rancor, in fact it left hardly a trace, and strange as it may seem, when we met at the lawyer's office, very soon after I left our home and returned to my parents', to destroy one of the two letters and start the annulment process with the other, he seemed so foreign to me, such a stranger, that it was hard to believe that I had slept in his bed so many nights, that I had awakened by his side so many mornings, that there had existed between us an intimacy that had brought us moments of rage and misfortune, but also others of extreme happiness, not a trace of which remained, maybe because around that time I had found you, and all the good and all the bad that had been done to me or that I had done to others no longer mattered, because everything had been swept clean and forgotten, because my life and my joy began with you.

And then, the first Sunday of August of that summer in which you had returned to Ithaca, my husband woke me up early—it could just as well have been eight in the morning as four in the afternoon—to inform me that he was leaving for the Costa Brava* and ask if I wanted to go with him, and the night before we had had a huge fight, about everything, about nothing, after which we had absurdly made love, and then returned with renewed verve to the contest, in a vicious circle that we could not or would not get out of—perhaps from the fear of plunging into a dreadful void—and which joined sex with aggression, so there was in our lovemaking a special intensity that we only attained after the frenzy of battle. But that morning, or that afternoon, I was exhausted and in a bad mood, and I turned over in bed and immediately went back to sleep, to awaken almost at nightfall, with a bitter taste in my mouth and a dull head. And even at sunset it was suffocatingly hot, a deadly sultry atmosphere, and I detest the heat, I detest the summer (unless I am on a boat or by the sea), I detest (or I did detest before I met you, because from that day on and for a long time it would acquire a special significance) the month of August, I have detested heart and soul and since infancy those terrible Sunday afternoons, not to mention Sunday afternoons in August in a feverish, deserted city. And all the friends I could fall back on were away for the weekend or for the summer vacation. And to top it off my husband had taken the car, which deprived me of the possibility of going to look for him at one of the fashionable spots along the coast and resuming with renewed gusto that exhausting game that once initiated, it seemed futile to try to free oneself from (his already being with another woman, which was more than likely, would have added a bit more spice and intensity to the new round of that stupid game), or of going somewhere alone. So I took a taxi, I left Sappho safe and sound at my parents' home, and asked to be taken to La Mariona, in the hopes of finding at the communal table people I was more or less acquainted with or a girlfriend with whom to begin passing the night, the *via crucis* of the night, which now, with the heat, did not end up at Jamboree but at an outdoor spot by the sea, where you could dance and drink and make out until dawn.

And at the shared table of the *gauche divine* there were only seven or eight people, but one of them was you, and my pulse quickened and I blessed the obstinacy of your wife in dragging you out with her, in taking you out in a group night after night. And someone, I don't remember who, got out a photography book that had just been published and laid it on the table, and we all got absorbed in it, and I was holding it with one hand, and you—I could not believe it, before your wife and those people and hardly knowing me—took my other hand beneath the table and held it tight for an eternity. And at that moment the world stopped, at least for me, it might as well have exploded in a thousand pieces, and the electric charge that passed from your skin to my skin was such that I was afraid I would fall dead or rise through the air like a new Mary Poppins* until my head hit the ceiling, if the roof did not open beforehand, as in the mystery of Elche,* to allow me, to allow the two of us, to ascend body and soul to the stars.

And I think it was you who proposed—and I doubt you had ever done so before that night—that we all go for drinks to the outdoor café by the sea, and there I went with you and your wife in your car. She did not tire of repeating that nothing made her jealous any more, that your constant infidelities had long since stopped mattering to her, that you were just staying together provisionally for the sake of the children, and I half believed her, because I am absurdly prone to believe whatever people say gratuitously and without anyone's asking them, but whether or not she said it, whether or not I believed it (it was obvious that the one who did not believe it was you) had no importance, because if you called me, and you were going to call me, I would go to you anyway, walking on water or pushing aside corpses, resolved to let—it is one of Christ's sayings that I prefer, and I wonder if I may be interpreting it wrong—the dead bury their dead.*

And on the dance floor, taking advantage of the fact that the orchestra was beginning an old slow and romantic number—I doubt your dancing abilities could have managed much more and we never danced together again nor did I see you dance with anyone else—you asked me to dance: that is to say, you led me to the center of the floor, where we were out of sight of our friends, and we stood there, in one another's arms and scarcely moving, like two dummies. And then, on that magical evening of a first Sunday of August, something unusual happened to me: if in the restaurant a while before I had felt myself levitate, now my body seemed to have turned to lead, I literally fainted from love—like the beloved in the Song of Songs* and without having friends there to fortify me with wine and apples—I was overcome by the weight of an extreme tension, everything started spinning around me—I think that if you had not held me up, I would have fallen to the floor and passed out—I felt light-headed as though I had had a pile of drinks and smoked a load of joints, and I discovered to my astonishment that one could, not as a metaphor but with the force of a physical phenomenon, fall ill from passion or love. So you accompanied me, concerned and a bit surprised—despite your reputation, it must not have happened often that women fainted like Doña Inés in your arms—your arm tightly wrapped around my waist, almost lifting me off the ground, to the ladies' room. I do not know if your wife and our friends saw us, if they inferred that I, usually so temperate, had really overdone it that night with drinks and marijuana, but none of that mattered anymore, because the rest of humanity had ceased to exist in that egoistic world in which there was only room for you and me. And I was throwing cold water on my face and moistening my temples with a foul eau de cologne that I found on the dressing table, while you waited for me outside, and then you put me into a taxi, and as I got in, I asked you, "When will we see each other again?", and you replied, "Every day for the rest of our lives." And I absolutely believed you, convinced that I had asked an idle question, out of the whim to hear you say out loud something I already knew, that both of us knew—without having any importance whatsoever the numerous village lasses, fisherwomen, novices, flight attendants, nymphs with golden tresses, friends of your wife, sorceresses and haughty princesses whom you had in turn loved and abandoned, hadn't I loved other men before meeting you?—that we were going to spend together every day of the rest of our lives, and that now, yes—on this occasion, yes—love would be a permanent calling, now, yes, until death did us part.

You left your home in mid-October (where, although you did not want to go into detail, life must have gotten very uncomfortable, because as soon as your wife suspected that there was again another woman and then the suspicion became a certainty and then she discovered that the other was I—it always seems to the wife, no matter what the situation, that the woman with whom her husband deceives her, or for whom he abandons her, is the worst of all possible options—her conviction suddenly vanished that she could no longer be jealous and that your marriage was finished) and moved into the room that an old couple was renting out because they could not live on the husband's pension, and who would not dream of turning on the heat or providing you with a stove when the winter cold set in. And soon after I would move back to my parents' home—I was delighted, you know, to temporarily regain my not so distant room and neighborhood and habits of

a single woman, including the waits by the telephone and the ren-
dezvous with my boyfriend at the entryway of the building or the corner bar—and we would start with Juan, by mutual consent, the annulment proceedings, which would include very infrequent interrogations
(in fact we did not do anything to speed them up and at times they had
to send us two or more subpoenas to testify, since he was in no rush to
marry again, and the idea would never again cross my mind, not with
you nor with anyone). So interrogations that were very spaced out (to
obtain nullity would take us nearly eight years), and indescribably
grotesque. What kind of farcical role was I playing there, in the then
grimy offices of the Church tribunal, explaining to a thin and seedy little old priest, with white stains on his black cassock, who got up more
and more often to go to the adjoining restroom—the sound of the toi-
let reached the table where I, demure and a little ashamed of so much
lying, was waiting for him—that I had studied from my early childhood
in one of the most elegant girls' schools in the city, Jesús María, which
was attended by true-blue middle-class girls, that I had stood out there
for my extreme piety and had been a fervent Daughter of Mary,* that I
had even considered entering the convent? (The letter that had been
destroyed was mine, because if it was necessary for the success of the
legal proceedings to have a victim to defend and a villain to accuse, the
lawyer had decided that I should be the virtuous one—it was always
more effective that the woman be the good one or the more stupid—
and Juan the bad guy of the movie.) What foolish part did I play, explaining that my love for Juan had arisen largely out of my zeal to re-
deem that Voltairean freethinking individual (who, according to the
annulment decree, "had already made manifest his outlandish beliefs
about the nature, purpose and dissolubility of marriage and had insinu-
ated his intention not to have offspring because children could be an
obstacle to his happiness"), whom I wished to return to the shepherd's
fold, that when I received from the hands of the maid, two hours before
the wedding ceremony, seated at my bedroom dressing table, where
the hairdresser was giving the final touches to my hairdo, and surrounded by my closest girlfriends, the letter in which my fiancé com-
municated to me his unyielding decision not to have children, I felt
myself die, I dissolved in tears, I wanted to call off the wedding ("the
impact this had on her was enormous"), but my friends convinced me
to ignore the letter, they assured me—they knew of several cases—that
after getting married and using with affection and cunning my femi-

nine charms, it would be easy to make him change his mind or confront him with *faits accomplis*; explaining that nonetheless, a lawyer friend of the family who had happened by chance to enter my bedroom, surreptitiously took the letter without anyone's noticing or my missing it, and had it authenticated that very day before a notary? (The incredible thing was not so much that they believed with remarkable naïveté this farfetched story, this improbable soap opera, as that the tribunal—represented on my side by the little old priest—only took into account in issuing its verdict the testimony of the two interested parties and their four or five chosen witnesses, when it would have sufficed to ask me for my school registration form or my marriage license, it would have been enough to make a few local phone calls—we were not before the Rota tribunal of Rome or Madrid,* but in Barcelona—to discover that I had not set foot for a single day in the school of Jesús María or any other religious school, that I had never been a Daughter of Mary—I would not even have been able to explain, if they had asked, what it consisted of or what duties and benefits came with being a member of the congregation of the Daughters of Mary—that my wedding had not been celebrated before the main altar of the cathedral, with a satin wedding gown and a tiara and a long train of tulle, and a profusion of flowers and lights and music, nor was it followed by a banquet with more than three hundred guests. Our fanciful lawyer would have loved to loop the loop of absurdity and present some photos of me dressed in my bridal gown, face contorted and eyes red from weeping, during the ceremony or upon leaving the church or at the banquet—gazing spellbound at the two rings of our clasped hands, cutting the enormous wedding cake, opening the dance with a waltz, throwing the bridal bouquet— but there was none of that, because we got married in street clothes, with no one present except our parents and the witnesses, in the side chapel of our parish church, without Mass, without a sermon, without flowers, without music and with hardly any light, and there was no banquet after the ceremony, and to top it off, that day I was, who knows why, happy as a lark, so we had to do without that eloquent documentary proof, because carrying the farce to the point of our disguising ourselves as the bridal couple, and Juan's faking haughty stubbornness and my faking desolate tears, to present some phony photos to the tribunal, seemed to me, to both of us, excessive.) What the devil was I doing there, telling the little old priest that after the wedding and contrary to my friends' predictions, everything had of course gone terribly

wrong, because Juan had persisted, without my tenderness and pleas
and feminine wiles—which must not have been so many—having any
effect at all, in employing means to prevent my getting pregnant?
("The hopes of the plaintiff were dashed from her very wedding night:
her husband never agreed to have natural marital relations and always
used means to prevent their having offspring.") Here the little priest
lowered his voice and asked me what had been those means, and the
scene reached its peak of grotesque obscenity, because he made an upward gesture with his hand, as though brushing away undesirable insects or dispersing seed, and he asked if Juan threw his semen outside,
and I answered yes, genuinely blushing from ear to ear. I told him that
we had fought more and more often and almost always for the same
reason, and without my achieving anything ("Don Juan did not put
aside his indomitable attitude even before the insistent pleas, demands
and even threats of his wife, who ardently desired to be a mother. This
stubborn opposition on the part of don Juan gave rise to constant and
serious quarrels between the couple"), and that I had returned a number of times to my parents' home, but Juan, although he continued to
be as Voltairean and freethinking as ever, always managed to convince
me to return to his side. "And how did he do that?" the priest then
asked, and I looked down as I answered, and I think this was the one
true statement out of that pack of lies, that he would send me a big bouquet of red roses, dozens of roses, with a card on which he had written,
"I love you." "And did you believe him?" the priest insisted. And I answered yes, or I half believed him or wanted to believe him, whereupon
the priest sadly and contritely shook his head and crossed himself over
the gullibility and naïveté of us women, he even admonished the girls
to whom he gave religion classes in the afternoons, telling them repeatedly: if you knew the things I hear in the curia in the mornings!
And I went on that finally I had to acknowledge that my marriage—
which in reality was not one, because the decision on the part of one
member of the couple not to have children automatically invalidates
the sacrament—had been a terrible mistake. ("Don Juan preferred sep-
aration from his wife—first from her bed and even table, and subse-
quently from home—to satisfying her in her legitimate desire to have
children.") And at that exact moment had appeared the lawyer friend of
my family who happened to be in my bedroom on the day of the wedding, as the hairdresser was putting the finishing touches on my hairdo,
and he had pulled out of his sleeve, as in a conjuring trick, now you see

it now you don't, the aforementioned letter that I thought was lost and of which I ignored the magical powers, having moreover been endorsed by a notary.

So that December we began processing the annulment, which after long spaced out and implausible interrogations—mine always alone with the little old priest in the dirty cassock—would be granted to us—with no other expenses, let it be said in the Church's honor, than the lawyers' and solicitors' fees—eight years later. I do not know if the ruse invented by our lawyer (a ruse that paradoxically contained, behind a pile of badly strung together lies that would not have withstood the slightest inquiry or the most benign analysis, a basic truth, because it was true that Juan and I had gotten married in the mutual agreement not to have children, which according to ecclesiastical law made the sacrament null and void) proliferated and was no longer effective, or if he invented—what a wasted talent for pulp novels or TV soap operas!—for each new case a different story, because it was obvious that you could not have many other couples appearing before the same tribunal, perhaps before the same little priest, with the identical script.

But while Juan and I were initiating a long struggle with the Church tribunal in which we did not have too much at stake, as for you, as if the problems you already had were not enough (the surprising thing was that nothing, not the letter in which your partner informed you that you had lost everything, nor the scenes most likely staged by your wife, nor the limitation of seeing your children at fixed hours—it was a shame that you could not see growing up at close range either them or the ones you would later have with me—nor working odd hours on badly paid jobs, nor the difficulties involved in readapting to a country you had been away from for so long, dampened your joy for having met me, for our loving each other and being together, and at that time it did not occur to me for a moment that playing such an enormous role in the life of another human being, substituting and compensating for so many lacks, so many frustrations, could in the long run become a trap for both of us), something happened to you which could have had grave consequences and which, I now think, did indeed. When you went to apply for a residence permit, the application was turned down: either you had to renounce Venezuelan citizenship or immediately leave the country, because they were not willing to run the risk of having someone with your political background remain in our country with the relative impunity of holding a foreign passport (in other words, they had allowed you to emigrate ages ago to the Americas, because they did not know what to do with you and it was an acceptable solution to keep you at a distance, and they had tolerated your spending the month of vacation here, but nothing in the course of all those years had expired or been forgotten, just as you had not forgotten the infernal circle of the release from and entry into the Montjuic prison, which could begin again). And then a right-wing friend—and not even from a civilized right wing, since he was on friendly terms with one of the most sinister henchmen of Francoism—whether because he liked you and secretly admired your success with women, the guts you had shown in politics, the ease with which you had earned money and the elegant generosity with which you had spent and lavished it on others, or because he was desperately trying to improve the image others had of him, or worse, that he had of himself, or because he was hoping that if the political situation changed in Spain, and it was apparent to all that in the not too distant future it would have to change, he could count on our returning the favor, accompanied you to the Central Police Headquarters and to some degree answered for you, he took the responsibility—and it was a bold act—for whatever you might do in the future—or rather, he promised that in the future you would do absolutely nothing—and thanks to his mediation, you came to a compromise, which was not, of course, a gentlemen's agreement that was morally binding, but a pact with a rogue whom you despised but who held your fate in his hands: you would give up your foreign passport and dual citizenship—that was nonnegotiable—but as long as you did not engage in any political activity whatsoever, nothing would happen to you. And for years, almost until the death of the Caudillo, you generally adhered to that pact, which bore an open threat, and it never occurred to me that you could behave otherwise (long afterwards, when the hatred you felt toward me equaled in intensity your love—not the love that I had inspired in you in the past, but that which remained alive within you, because no one has ever loved me or hated me as much as you—when I turned into the great culprit, you would also accuse me of this, of having kept you away from the political struggle, but the fact is that neither did the comrades who had fought with you years before or who were fighting in the opposition then ever allow you to take part in activities in which, it seemed to me and to them, you would have vainly risked more than others), but if I try to understand what happened later between us, I think that that prolonged mutilation of such an important part of yourself (maybe since at the age of ten you threw confetti from the balcony celebrating the advent of the Republic), during years when you were gradually losing interest in many other things, that forced immobility at a time when the country was finally starting to awaken from its lethargy—and even I, without running any risk worthy of mention, was signing protest documents, taking part in occasional demonstrations or joining in sit-ins with artists and intellectuals in a monastery or convent: was occupying what you felt was your place—was probably another of the factors that in the long run I had, the two of us had, against us.

The Monday that followed that first Sunday in August we met at the entryway of my parents' home, and when you asked me where I wanted to go and I answered anywhere where we could be alone, you looked surprised, although just for a few seconds, and I asked laughing, "Do you think we need some kind of courtship? that we should wait a few days? that we should at least go first to a bar to chat and have some drinks?", and you laughed too, and I think that for the second time we felt sure—the first time had occurred the night before, when you said "Every day for the rest of our lives" and I believed you—that this was not a question of one more affair, that something extraordinary was about to happen or was already happening to us, which all the same was rather curious, given the great fame you enjoyed as an incorrigible womanizer and given the fact that I was going through a stage (the first of my life, because despite my passionate adolescent loves and my loudly proclaimed nonconformity and having grown up in a rather unconventional bourgeois family, the rigid customs imposed jointly by the Franco dictatorship and the Catholic Church, reinforced by the fear of becoming pregnant, had kept me chaste much longer than I was willing to admit) of relative promiscuity.

Although the phenomenon had not reached the countries of Latin America and did not concern you (in fact you must have considered us, or considered them, rich kids and snobs, and must not have understood why one needed so much ideological underpinning, so much artifice and group consciousness to do something that you had been freely practicing and without other conflicts than the jealousy of your wife or of your lovers' husbands ever since you were deflowered joyously and without trauma at the age of fourteen by your mother's best friend; so that when you and I talked about sex, which did not happen often, and we both declared ourselves to be fervent believers in sexual freedom, we did not share, although at the time I was unaware of this, exactly the same attitude), we were living through the magnificent and crazy and controversial and in any case unique and stimulating sixties, years in which people did not yet know about AIDS but the birth control pill was arriving in Spain; in which we took seriously and literally the slogan "Make love, not war"—which the most prestigious, committed and snobbish Italian publisher would change to "Fate l'amore, no l'editore";* in which sex as a game and political progressivism seemed to us, to the later outrage of the feminists, who only saw in pornography another manifestation of male chauvinism, to go hand in hand, and we all returned from Perpignan* with the latest issues of the *Ruedo Ibérico** and *Playboy* hidden together in the bottom of the suitcase, and returned from Paris after seeing politically *engagé* cinema, films like *To Die in Madrid* or *Night and Fog* or *The Battleship Potemkin*, and with the same diligence, as though obeying a moral imperative, the Jeanne Moreau of *Les amants* or the striptease show at Crazy Horse;* in which the actors of the Living Theater—which, due to a rare censorial oversight, maybe because the production was in English and had the title of an apparently innocuous Greek tragedy, could give two memorable performances in Barcelona that were attended by our clan en masse—went around the stage repeating the transgressive and sacred gesture—strangely enough very similar to that of the little priest of the Church tribunal, except that in him it was obscene and vulgar, while here it was not—of enthusiastically throwing the presumed semen in the air, as they chanted something like "You can't have a revolution without a great copulation";* years in which one started the night at La Mariona and followed it up at Jamboree and somewhat later at Bocaccio,* without knowing for sure—and it was an exciting uncertainty—in what bed you would end up, nor with whom, nor of which sex; in which, in the words of the opinionated female poet who had just discovered Virginia Woolf and in a display of fantasy linked Bloomsbury to the Vallès,* every time they introduced you to someone and you shook his hand, you were assessing how he would be as a lover; in which one of the prominent architects of the group—who assured us that the queen of England was the best dressed woman in the world and whose girlfriend was so sophisticated that she subsisted on a diet of clams and café con leche—received us at one of his wild and Fellinesque parties* kissing all the women on the navel, to make, he assured us, the enthusiasm that he felt for our faces and our breasts and our backs gradually descend to the more obscure zones that lie below the waist of the female body—Lord, how idiotic the idea must have seemed to you!; in which some men and women kept in mind a list of celebrities they intended to screw someday and made note of each conquest in an imaginary or real datebook, emulating the notches the cowboys of the Wild West would etch on their revolver for every man they killed; years in which the wife of a publisher poet, a charming, well-educated little bourgeoise, kindly asked the guests she did not know well enough upon assigning them rooms to spend the night in her home, "Hetero? Homo?"; although I have to admit that this living sex as a moral imperative, and this inbred amatory frenzy, and this freedom never before practiced in the somber Spain of the post-Civil War, did not prevent its happening on occasion, only on occasion, that the wives who considered themselves betrayed made a colossal scene in public, or appeared in the living room with the veins of their wrists slit, a trail of blood spoiling the Persian or designer rug, or that the men who considered themselves deceived—even though there was no deception whatsoever, because it all unfolded in broad daylight and with general approval, the term "cuckold" did not disappear—chased the unfaithful wife brandishing a kitchen knife, or kicked to pieces the furniture of the apartment, also designer furniture, and smashed on the floor the clay whistle dolls* that were one of the anagrams of modernity.

So it was curious that, with your being a womanizer of the old school, and my participating to some degree in the promiscuous and tumultuous sixties, in which we lived sex as a game and as a political cause, it did not occur to us that our relationship could be limited to one more affair, an incidental fling, and this was because for the first time in my life, and perhaps also in yours, love had welled up spontaneously, mutual and complete, and we advanced toward one another as though we were the only real inhabitants of a planet suddenly peopled only by shadows—mobile figures in technicolor against an immobile black-and-white background—as though there did not exist any reality as sure or as important as that which was being born between the two of us: we knew that there would not be a courtship on your part, nor genuine or feigned resistance on mine, that no one was seducing anyone, that there was not going to be one person who loved more and another who let himself be loved, that neither of us would clumsily try to maintain his sphere of power or to control a magical experience that had been given to us and surpassed us, that it would be a total surrender, without conditions or meanness or reservations, that on this occasion we had not put anything away for safekeeping nor hung up our clothes before plunging hand in hand into the most tempestuous part of the torrent ("tempestuous" was one of the words you loved and I never say or write it without thinking of you), nor had we neglected to burn the smallest of our ships and even the lifeboat in the event that we failed in the endeavor, we knew that we had both given ourselves with all we were and all we possessed into the hands of the other, that we had lowered our guard, that we were betting it all on one number, and either we would win the jackpot or end up helpless and needy in the most wild, impenetrable part of the forest, lost and naked in the dark night, and I thought much later, when I had to pay a price, that we should have been terrified, but we were not, because we were a pair of fools and because deep within us and for a long time—not, oh what sorrow, not, as I then believed, for all our lives—there was only room for ecstatic love and for the most extreme happiness.

We made love for the first time on that first Monday of August, in the house of call chosen by the taxi driver, and it turned out surprisingly easy and simple, devoid of artifice—no one would have guessed it was a question of an experienced Don Juan and a lewd lass of the sixties—maybe because we did not have anything to prove—I felt and would feel for years fully accepted by you, in a way that I had never before and would never again feel accepted by any man—or the slightest sensation of seducing the other or taking an exam, and you did not ask me the futile question, since I have always been too polite or too discreet or too afraid to hurt the other's feelings to answer in the negative or even evasively, whether I enjoyed it, nor deemed me a marvel, a goddess in bed (some time later you would tell me, and this must have been true, that you had never met a woman who made love so joyfully), nor did you make the absurd claim of doing something with me that no one else had done in that specific way and that would mark me forever. And yet, months would pass—we were already living together—before I discovered to my amazement that there was much about my own sexuality—so inclined in recent times to erotic games, so dedicated to making love, not war—that I ignored, that there was a specific kind of pleasure that I was completely unaware of and had not sought with you or with any man prior to you because not only did I not know what it consisted of or how to attain it, but even that it existed, a dimension of enjoyment for which my body—the body always wiser, always surer and more subtle than what we call spirit—had been patiently waiting for you, and I did not say anything to you about it—I who at that time told you everything, because you were interested in any trifle related to me—for weeks I strove not to reveal anything, because I was embarrassed that at that stage of life, with so many notches on the butt of my revolver (which in fact were not so many) and so much erotic sophistication, I had just discovered something so simple.

And there began a period of exalted happiness, not just moments of happiness as I had known in the past, but happiness as an almost permanent state of being, as a scarcely interrupted ecstasy, so intense and so intoxicating that no difficulty, no setback managed to tarnish it for long. Being by your side, seeing you, hearing you, touching you was a feast for the soul and for the senses, and if for me loneliness did not literally begin two steps away from you, like that of the water nymph and the enamored fish of Giraudoux,* it is true that it began when you were not present, and that there was an aura around you that seemed to preserve me from all harm, that dispelled ancestral anxieties and fears, that portended immortality, or at least made death into something distant and implausible, because love was stronger than death when you held me in your arms, or simply when part of my body was in contact with yours. And I rediscovered by your side new forms of tenderness, new nuances of flavor, new meanings for old words: with you I rediscovered the world of the simple things as though it had just been created or as though I had just been born.

Even being short of money, far from tingeing our daily life with squalor, for me became a game. Before we could live together, I would wait for you at noon at the entrance to your workplace, go with you to a bar where we were regulars and they treated us kindly, and watch you eat (it was fantastic to see you eat, just as it would be fantastic and moving later on, when we spent the entire night together, to see you sleeping, although yours was often a restless sleep and I was not able to come up with a gentle enough way of waking you to avoid your giving a start with a brusque defensive gesture, like a lone ranger or a guerilla fighter whom an enemy could surprise in the middle of the night and immediately reaches for a nonexistent pistol), as I sipped a Coca-Cola slowly, to make it last (you invariably protested against the depravity of ingesting that odious Yankee brew instead of drinking a decent glass of good wine), and afterwards I went to have a free meal at my parents' home, while you resumed your work. At night we did manage to eat together somewhere—although we could rarely pay for a room in a house of call or a hotel—and then took a long stroll through the streets of the neighborhood, with no destination, delaying the moment in which we would have to part, in a tight embrace, I leaning against you and objecting to the imaginary cold of the autumn night, to end up laughing open-mouthed—like poor children before the show window of a pastry shop—before a furniture store where they had on display on the other side of the mirror, totally beyond our reach, a magnificent wedding bed with a satin bedspread and a high canopy. And later on we would subsist for weeks at a time on spaghetti, rice with a fried egg and spicy pork sausage—unless some friend generously invited us out for a sirloin steak—but this did not stop me from appearing some day with two dozen oysters and a bottle of good wine, or stop us from tightening our belts to the limit and then taking off for a few days in Paris, I being convinced, like Wilde,* that one can do without everything in life except the superfluous, and you ready to share in all my whims.

Then time passed—four or five years perhaps—and on an indeterminate day, or on a long series of indeterminate days, I found that my pulse no longer quickened when you entered the room, that it no longer took my breath away when you placed a hand on me or gave me a kiss, nor was a night without you a sleepless night, nor a few days without you an unending hell; I discovered that my recurrent fantasy, so literary moreover, that an impenetrable forest would spring up around us, like that surrounding the palace of Princess Aurora,* and that without further delay eternity would begin for the two of us, alone together forever, could turn out, if it were granted (and you threatened to make it real, because we went to less and less places and saw fewer and fewer people, you were ever more reluctant to go anywhere and were irritated by an ever growing number of people, especially my people, in whom you had begun to see a danger), a bit claustrophobic; that I no longer raved with anxiety—as I later would with our children—if you arrived home or for an appointment a little late, nor rushed to imagine the thousand accidents that might have befallen you, including an abduction by extraterrestrials; that the show windows of the stores were no longer just places to display objects that might be useful to you or you might like; that books, shows, travel had stopped being by definition experiences to be shared with you, that I could only fully enjoy if you were by my side, because Paris would still be Paris, and the Seine would not alter its course, they would not even have replaced the receptionist of our hotel or the baskets of oysters before our favorite restaurants have disappeared, and Venice would still be Venice, and even the Tetrarchs, whom we had chosen as privileged witnesses of our bliss in a magical city, and to whom we made on every trip—I have continued making without you—a ritual visit, offered a farewell greeting, would remain in the same corner, immobile and foreign between the Basilica of Saint Mark and the Doge's Palace, and the Bellinis at Harry's Bar and the cappuccinos at the Florian* would taste the same without you (maybe we were not, it came to me as a revelation, the first lovers to cross those bridges or sail through those canals); I admitted sadly that there were other realities on earth more important than love, the grand love that we had constructed—or that had been graciously bestowed on us—between the two of us, and that perhaps this love was not so unique or exceptional over the course of time; I realized that love was not, for me or for anyone, except in magnificent and deceptive interludes, stronger than death, and that there was around me a multitude of different men and women, with whom I could never live something similar to what I had lived with you, but who promised me a thousand different stories, that I had no reason to refuse, that you—although at that time you often failed to recognize it—had no right to prohibit me or prohibit yourself from, because if for so long we had limited ourselves to one another, it was, at least in my case, because there did not exist in the world any other human being who could be the object of my desire or simply of my curiosity, not because monogamy or marital fidelity had any place whatever in our moral code, either mine or yours. After four or five years there came a moment—or a series of imprecise moments, as occurs with the first symptoms of a physical pain or illness, when we are not aware at what moment they started or at what moment we perceived them—when I realized with desolation—you cannot even imagine with what degree of desolation—that I was no longer in love with you: I continued to be very fond of you, you were the most marvelous thing that had ever happened to me, but I was no longer in love with you, and that falling out of love was as foreign to my will, as spontaneous and as inevitable as had been my earlier love.

I have often wondered, and we will never know, if (despite the cataclysm that fell upon us, despite the fact that the fear of losing me unleashed in you a boundless fury—the more intense for being irrational—and transformed what had been the most joyous and generous and tender of emotions into a morbid, lethal passion—lethal for both of us, but more so for you—because perhaps in the last analysis love was not stronger than death, but as I discovered dumbfounded, jealousy was indeed worse than death) something similar to what was happening to me was at that time incubating in you, if within you was also disappearing that raving love, that absolute romantic love that leaves no room for anything else and that would be hard put to last us until death, to be transformed into a different, calmer feeling; I have wondered whether, if the evolution was similar in the two of us, we might have been able, by lowering the register of our story, reducing the sum total of the bet, to continue living together, and if this would have been better or worse for the two of us.

What is certain is that together we traversed all the circles of heaven and hell, that we were happy and wretched as we had never been before and probably never would be again, that we loved and hated each other beyond rhyme or reason, that we said to each other the most tender and the most atrocious words, that we did to each other all the good and all the bad that was within our grasp. Until one day, more solitary than ever, more bitter, more furious, you admitted the defeat—your defeat and my defeat—you boarded your phantom ship—the only vessel that had survived the torching of the fleet—you gave orders to your crew of specters, you unfurled your black sails in the wind and set out to sea. And I remained on shore, sad and distressed, feeling a bit guilty for not having been equal to Senta, but also a certain relief—the relief one feels when someone you love very much finally dies, after a long and painful illness for which there does not exist a cure—and I was not capable of hurling myself like Senta into the sea from the height of the rocky cliffs, crying out the redeeming words, the words that make possible the definitive triumph of love: "Here am I, faithful to you unto death."

Epilogue

Y ES, THERE WERE INTERESTING MEN AND WOMEN AROUND ME, WHO
offered the prospect of different experiences, and I lived some of them.
Hadn't I let my Flying Dutchman, so long awaited and who for years
filled to overflowing all my expectations, leave, and hadn't I—so given
to grand gestures—relinquished the idea of throwing myself after him
into the waves and swearing loyalty to him beyond death, but instead
had remained on shore, distressed and a little ashamed for not being
equal to Senta, but also secretly relieved? Hadn't I resolved never again
to live with someone as a couple, in part because I was sure that if it had
not gone well on this occasion it would not yield better results with any
other man, but also in part to be able to freely and openly—far from
being stimulating, secrecy has always bothered and inhibited me—experience them? And some turned out beautiful or entertaining or tender or even at moments passionate; others foolish or sordid; some
ended badly and others I don't even recall any more how they ended;
and others led to an affectionate and lasting friendship. And in many of
them I invented in part—don't we all?—the object of desire; I embel-
lished and distorted—often knowingly—the stark reality, although love
would never constitute for me a solitary endeavor or game.

But something had changed. I stopped living stories, and began to
just experience things. It was not a question that in my early forties I
considered myself finished for affairs of the heart, nor that I was inhibited by the fear of no longer being able to please: it was something
deeper and more intimate and that would prove irreversible. In my
early forties there rose around me, if not a glass bell (it was by no means
so dramatic, in fact it was not at all dramatic), if not a dense forest like
that of Princess Aurora (in my fantasies there had never been a place,
since I left girlhood behind, for Prince Charmings who would awaken
me with a kiss and carry me off to their kingdom on their white horse),
yes an ever more closely woven veil, although difficult to detect, that di-

117

minished the colors of things, that depleted my capacity for enthusiasm, the ability to lower my guard—hadn't the two of us, Esteban and I,
paid such a high price for doing this?—to give myself entirely to anyone
or anything, to—and I had considered myself the most amorous of
creatures, I recalled myself captivated by someone since the most distant childhood, I had subscribed to the assertion of Victor Hugo: "Je
n'ai rien plus à faire ici bas que d'aimer"*—fall in love again. I stopped,
for better or for worse, taking such a literary view of life, of mine and
others', I stopped dressing it in the trappings of melodrama (or at least
did so less), it became more difficult for me to attain, always in company
(although it did not necessarily have to be in the company of a lover or
of a close living being, it could be with Brassens,* who in the first and
most passionate period with Esteban was on at full volume for hours, as
we moved intoxicated around the apartment flooded with light; with
Piaf, so moving, so insignificant, so immense, in one of her last performances at the Olympia;* with the Assyrian reliefs at the British Museum,* that catch and hold me transfixed and never allow me to go to
the second floor to complete the visit to the museum; with some Egyptian temples at a magical twilight hour, and better still if you approach
them by felucca;* with the sunrise on Cap de Creus* and the first dip in
the virgin, icy water; with so many movies and theatrical productions of
Visconti,* of Bergman [I cannot express here as Bergman does in *Wild
Strawberries** the nostalgia and sadness of growing old in a world gradually peopled more and more with phantoms]; with Béjart: that incom-
parable *Rites of Spring** that brought me to my feet for minutes, ap-
plauding and crying, at a time when I did not yet stupidly cry over
everything; with some moments of the *Faust* of Strehler,* the *Antigone*
of the Living Theater,* the voice of Berta Singerman, the sculptures of
the Medici Chapels,* or the Parthenon* seen at a distance, from the
balcony of the hotel where I was having breakfast with my children), so
never alone, then, the seventh heaven, or to believe that I had attained,
never alone, the deepest circle of hell, where lovelessness resides. I
stopped seeing myself as a romantic heroine who was living exceptional
stories; I stopped taking myself so seriously and considering myself the
center, not only of the big wide world, in which I have always known
myself to be less significant than a grain of sand, but of my own tiny
world, among other reasons because the center of my own tiny world
had come to be occupied irrevocably by my children, with whom I have
shared many things and who have given me loads of happiness, but for

whom I have felt and feel something that has little or nothing to do with romantic love and passion. And nonetheless, if on the other side of the dense veil reality had lost brilliance and intense coloring, in contrast, far from getting blurry, it gained sharper contours, more precise, exact lines, and my gaze became wiser, more understanding, kinder, and above all more ironic (I resist saying more mature).

Also in my early forties I started to become conscious—as I think everyone does, although I do not know if it happens at the same moment or by the same paths, or if it always, as in my case, becomes obsessive—of the limitations imposed on us by the passage of time. I observed that the wide spectrum of possibilities open to us during adolescence and youth had been shrinking, had inexorably folded up like the ribs of a fan, and that every choice brought in its wake a host of renunciations. During the first moments, in the first stage, one considers the innumerable things that one has dreamed about and now knows definitely one is never going to do or know or enjoy. Later on, in a second stage, there arises the uncertainty as to how long one will be able to continue knowing, enjoying and experiencing what one still knows, enjoys and experiences. Not only friendships to preserve or start, loves to maintain or initiate, books to write, but trifles that become day by day more important. Future dogs, whom I can only take charge of if I assume that I will live long enough to take care of them until their end, or if I know of someone who if need be could replace me; beautiful objects, old books, rare books that give me so much pleasure, that constitute an important part of my life, but that lately I acquire taking into account if one of my children also likes them, or what museum or library I will leave them to; journeys that entail some physical exertion, and that I do not know until when I will be capable of; the next car I am going to buy and which may be the last one I own and drive . . . My friend Adela outdoes me and loops the loop saying that she does not even buy green fruit any more, for fear she will not have time to see it ripen.

Starting in my early forties I have felt—do we all feel?—that time, at that stage in which we no longer live stories but simply go through things, slips ever faster—gold dust, trickling water—through our fingers, and although I know it is beyond my strength to prevent it, at times I have felt and feel as though I am to blame, as though time were passing so very fast through my own carelessness, because I have not applied myself enough or been clever enough to retain it. So that, on the second day of a trip or vacation or the visit of a beloved friend, I begin keeping a strict count of the days that remain. And for many years I have had a recurrent dream, perhaps my only recurrent dream. I am in a village on the shore of the same sea as all my summers (for how many more summers? hasn't it already happened to me on many occasions to do something habitual for the last time without having the slightest premonition that it would be the last time? didn't Marsé* explain that the future has no existence whatsoever, that the present exists only a little and the only thing that really exists is the past?), with my children and with friends (there often appear in the dream friends who are no more, who will never again go down to the Marítim* at nightfall to see the unbelievable color that inundates the town and tinges the sea at a certain hour, who will not light for me [who do not smoke] a ritual cigarette, upon getting on the boat after a swim, nor open a bottle of white wine upon returning home at noon while the others are taking a shower, nor play cards with me until dawn, nor force me to watch on television by their side the Tour de France),* and incredibly it's the last day of vacation, and we have to return to the city, and I wonder and ask the others in despair, desolate and furious, because I feel cheated by the universal approval, how is it possible that we have not set sail a single time, that they have not even put the boat in the water—Tururut, the little boat designed by my father, discussing every detail one by one with the builder, the last wooden boat that was made in the village— that these most precious and perhaps unrepeatable weeks have been lost? So that, in real life (or in what I keep on considering to be real life), I stubbornly insist—and I know it is a childish insistence—on going out sailing every day, even when it's raining cats and dogs or the north wind is blowing fiercely or a southwest wind threatens, although I know for a fact that it is futile, because the end will always come and will leave me frustrated, since there will always be something that I failed to do, or that I could not do, or that I could have done but did not do, or that I did indeed do but did not afford me the degree of pleasure anticipated, the degree of pleasure I deserved (and who owed it to me? and isn't it stupid this feeling that I do not enjoy myself enough, that I do not pay enough attention to the things I love or that I remember having loved not so long ago?).

And I discovered long since that what matters, what is at stake, is not a summer vacation, or a trip, or a sojourn in one of the cities I love, or even the fleeting presence by my side of a loved one who lives on the

other side of the world: what matters is that these repeated and inex-
orable endings, this sensation of loss, are simply a metaphor, advance
premonitory images of the most certain and most implausible—or has
it become with old age less implausible and less feared and almost acceptable?—of truths: that sooner or later we are all going to die.

Starting in my forty-some years, perhaps from the moment when I
let my Flying Dutchman set sail without me in his ship with the black
sails and ghostly crew, from the moment when I stopped living stories
and started just experiencing things—some pleasant, some gratifying,
some that have made me happy—nostalgia and sadness, which should
not be confused with the apathy and melancholy that had been on my
trail forever (I remember at the age of six or seven, dying of longing for
my classmates and teacher and even the classroom and desk of the previous year; crying inconsolably at the end of every school year; so
gloomy and upset at the end of a party at home that since early childhood my mother allowed a girlfriend to stay overnight, so I would not
feel abandoned and lost amid the half-empty glasses of tiger nut milk—
later of Coca-Cola and sangria—the crumpled-up paper napkins and
awful remains of sandwiches and pastries), caught up with me and
gradually settled within me: if the only thing that really exists is the
past, how can we escape nostalgia? how can we elude sadness at a time
when colors are fading, when life closes to us a range of possibilities
that we had fantasized as almost infinite, and when the future exists less
from day to day? That is why I spend more and more time, and with
touches of morbidity, roaming the spots where I lived in my childhood
and youth. I make a pilgrimage to the places where I spent my earliest
years (not long ago I read somewhere the statement: "We always feel
nostalgia for the places where we were young," and it seemed revealing
to me that the person being interviewed [I do not even remember who
it was] said "where we were young" and not "where we were happy").
And this is the fundamental reason why I would not be able to live in a
city other than my own, the city where the most things have happened
to me; this is the reason why any other city would be tantamount to
exile. And I seek reunions with old friends who are still alive—still
many, still, but for how long, most of them—and they tell me about the
illnesses and scholastic achievements of their grandchildren, that they
were in London and it seemed to them very dirty, they tell me about
the advantages of their upcoming retirement, and I do not dare protest
that the illnesses and successes of grandchildren whom I hardly know

do not matter to me in the least, I can't bring myself to reply that London is to me a beautiful city and I have never noticed that it was dirty, that plans for retirement seem to me absurd (wasn't it just yesterday that we were trying to make headway in our professional life?), that what I am really seeking, what I want from them, is to revive shreds of a shared past (with every loved one who dies, whom we somehow or other lose, escape from us pieces of our own life, so I cry as much for myself as for them), sometimes more real, often more multicolored, than what is happening to us now, the recovery of a lost time that I fear I am unable to bring safely home without their help.

Until upon reaching the end—an end that in my youth seemed terrifying, in maturity roused me to rebel, but that I am now close to accepting—when the final curtain falls and I make my final exit from the scene, there converge in one point the past, the present and the future, and my broken, frayed stories come to swell the vast torrent that flows into the common sea of all stories.

Glossary

Page references in this volume precede each note.

(28) *my brother . . . his first book*: Oscar Tusquets (1941–), Catalan architect and interior designer. The book is entitled *Más que discutible: Observaciones dispersas sobre el arte como disciplina útil* (1994).

(28) *Gorgon*: A female monster in Greek mythology, whose hair was made of snakes and whose hideous face had the power to turn the onlooker into stone.

(28) *the first lady of Olympus or Valhalla*: In Greek mythology, Hera, queen of the gods, lived with Zeus, king of the gods, on Mount Olympus, the official abode of the divinities. In German and Old Norse mythology, Frea (or Frigg; Fricka in Wagner's *Ring* cycle), queen of the gods, and Wodan (or Odin; Wotan in Wagner's cycle), king of the gods, resided in the castle Valhalla, the "Hall of the Slain," a paradise for brave warriors who died in battle.

(29) *Civil War*: The Spanish Civil War (1936–39), pitting the left-wing Republicans against the conservative Nationalists under General Francisco Franco (1892–1975). After the Nationalist victory, Franco headed a fascist military dictatorship, remaining in power until his death.

(30) *FAI*: Federación Anarquista Ibérica, a loosely knit federation of anarchist groups in Spain and Portugal, established in 1927. Wishing to arouse the masses to revolution, they organized three uprisings in 1932 and 1933, all of which were unsuccessful.

(30) *the princess and the pea*: "The Princess and the Pea" (1835), a fairy tale by the Danish author Hans Christian Andersen (1805–75).

(31) *Catalonia*: Northeastern region of Spain bordering on the French Pyrenean frontier and the Mediterranean Sea; the capital is Barcelona. The most prosperous and highly industrialized part of Spain, it has its own language (Catalan) and vibrant cultural life.

(32) *Zola, Balzac, and Voltaire*: Emile Zola (1840–1902), late nineteenth-century French writer of the naturalist school, author of the twenty-novel series *Les Rougon-Macquart*. Honoré de Balzac (1799–1850), French realist author who penned the vast fictional panorama of contemporary French society *La comédie humaine*. Voltaire, pseudonym of François-Marie Arouet (1694–1778), French enlightenment author and

philosopher who promoted reason over the blind acceptance of authority, using his wit to satirize and attack the Church and other traditional institutions in favor of religious tolerance and freedom of thought and action.

(32) *the Sacred Heart . . . Leonardo*: A Roman Catholic devotion to the physical heart of Jesus, symbolizing divine love for humanity; an image of the Sacred Heart is placed in the home, and a priest or head of household consecrates the family members to the Sacred Heart. Leonardo da Vinci (1452–1519), Italian artist, sculptor, draftsman, architect, and engineer whose brilliance embodied the Renaissance humanist ideal; his paintings include the *Mona Lisa* and the *Last Supper*.

(32) *The Perfect Wife*: *La perfecta casada* (1583), a prose work by the Spanish Renaissance poet cleric Fray Luis de León (1528–91) in which he expounds his view of the qualities and duties of the ideal Christian wife.

(33) *Scheherazade*: The legendary queen of the *Arabian Nights' Entertainment*, wife of the Sultan Shahriyar of Persia. The Sultan had the practice of strangling his wives after the wedding night, but he spared her life because she entertained him with her suspenseful chain of stories.

(33) *the third brother*: A common paradigm found in many traditional fairy tales; some examples from the Brothers Grimm are "The Golden Goose," "The Water of Life," and "The Poor Miller's Boy and the Cat."

(33) *Siegfried*: A heroic prince of German and Old Norse literature, whose exploits included winning the treasure hoard of the Nibelung.

(33) *Valkyrie*: Brunhilde (Brünnhilde in Wagner's *Ring* cycle), daughter of Wodan, an Amazon-like princess in ancient Germanic literature. In some sources she was a Valkyrie, one of a group of supernatural maidens on horseback who served Wodan by carrying off dead warrior heroes to Valhalla.

(35) *The Anatomy Lesson*: *The Anatomy Lesson of Dr. Nicolaes Tulp* (1632), a painting by Rembrandt van Rijn (1606–69), outstanding Dutch seventeenth-century painter, draftsman, and etcher.

(35) *Bauhaus*: Innovative German school of architecture, design, and arts that existed from 1919 to 1933, founded by the architect Walter Gropius; it aimed to manufacture functional and aesthetically pleasing products for the masses rather than individual objects for an affluent elite.

(36) *Phryne*: Famous Athenian courtesan of the fourth century B.C., who served as the model for Praxiteles' nude sculpture the Cnidian Aphrodite.

(37) *Wagnerian opera*: Richard Wagner (1813–83), German dramatic composer whose operas and other works had a profound impact on the history of Western music. He used German and Norse legends and myths as the basis for his great operatic tetralogy *The Ring of the Nibelung* (1869–76).

(37) *Gunther*: A warrior king in old Germanic literature; in the twelfth-century epic *The Nibelungenlied* he is the king of Burgundy. Siegfried betrays Brunhilde by aiding

Gunther in winning her, and in return marrying Gunther's sister Kriemhilde (Gutrune in Wagner's *Ring* cycle).

(37) *Brunhilde*: In both Old Norse and German sources, Brunhilde vows to marry only a man of superior qualities and one who exceeds her in strength. Siegfried is the only man who can satisfy her conditions, but he does not win her for himself but for another. Upon realizing the deception Brunhilde takes her revenge, leading to the death of Siegfried.

(37) *Colegio Alemán*: The German School, a private German secondary school located in Esplugues de Llobregat, Barcelona; founded in 1894.

(38) *Chiparus*: Art deco sculptures by the Romanian sculptor Dimitri Chiparus (1888–1950). He emigrated to Paris where he studied with Antonin Mercier and Jean Boucher, creating dramatic, stylized figures of bronze and ivory.

(40) *Andalusia*: The southernmost region of Spain, facing both the Atlantic Ocean and the Mediterranean Sea; a stronghold of Moorish culture in the Middle Ages.

(40) *duro*: Spanish five-peseta coin; the peseta is the basic monetary unit of Spain.

(43) *Cervantes*: Miguel de Cervantes Saavedra (1547–1616), Spanish Golden Age novelist, playwright, and poet, author of *Don Quijote de la Mancha* (1605, 1615); regarded as the greatest figure in Spanish literature.

(45) *plain, Catholic, and sentimental*: In the subtitle of chapter 2 there is a playful allusion to the protagonist of the *Sonatas* (1902–5), a series of novels by the early twentieth-century Spanish author Ramón del Valle-Inclán (1866–1936). In an introductory note to the *Sonatas*, the author describes the protagonist, the Marquis of Bradomín, as an admirable Don Juan because he is "plain, Catholic, and sentimental" [*feo, católico y sentimental*].

(45) *Quevedo . . . Antonio Machado*: Francisco Gómez de Quevedo y Villegas (1580–1645), Golden Age poet, satirist, and novelist known for his sharp wit and brilliant use of the Spanish language. Garcilaso de la Vega (1503–36), the first important poet of the Golden Age of Spanish literature (c. 1500–1650); he adapted the meter of Italian Renaissance poetry to Spanish to write expressive analytical poems, often laments, on the vicissitudes of romantic love. Antonio Machado (1875–1939), major Spanish poet and playwright of the Generation of 1898; he is especially known for his poetry of the second period such as *Campos de Castilla* [*The Lands of Castile*] (1912), in which he portrayed in an austere and gloomy style the stark countryside and spirit of Castile.

(45) *Gabriel y Galán . . . José María Pemán*: José María Gabriel y Galán (1870–1905), poet from Salamanca who wrote spontaneous but tritely sentimental regional poetry exalting Spanish country life. Ramón de Campoamor y Campoosorio (1817–1901), post-Romantic poet from Asturias who expounded a new conception of poetry in his theoretical treatise *Poética* (1883), but whose poetry did not live up to his own precepts, being for the most part only shallow philosophical verses of affected simplicity. José María Pemán (1898–1981), popular Spanish dramatist and poet of the 1930s through 1970s from Cádiz, with a generally benign, traditionalist view of life.

(45) *Verdi . . . Strauss*: Giuseppe Verdi (1813–1901), nineteenth-century Italian opera composer who transformed the *bel canto* tradition by expanding the use of the orchestra while still giving lyrical primacy to the singers, all with the aim of serving the drama. Giacomo Puccini (1858–1924), turn-of-the-century Italian opera composer whose works epitomized operatic realism. Richard Strauss (1864–1949), German late Romantic composer known for his symphonic poems and operas; his works came out of the Wagnerian Romantic tradition while blending in a delicate Mozartean sensibility.

(45) *Avignon*: Ancient city in southeastern France on the Rhône River. A stronghold of the Gauls, then a Roman city; capital of the papacy in the fourteenth century.

(48) *Sagrado Corazón . . . Santa Elizabeth*: Select Catholic girls' schools in Barcelona.

(48) *satanic and lecherous priest . . . nun*: A reference to Martin Luther (1483–1546), founder of the sixteenth-century Protestant Reformation. Luther sought to reform the Catholic Church by attacking its abuses, such as the issuance of "indulgences" which the sinner could buy to commute the punishment for his sins, and papal "bulls" or edicts. He married a former nun, Katherina von Bora, in 1525.

(49) *"El dos de mayo" . . . war*: "The Second of May" (1866), a patriotic ode on the 1808 Madrid uprising against the French Napoleonic invasion, by the Spanish poet Bernardo López (1840–70). The lines in the original are: *Guerra clamó ante el altar el sacerdote con ira, guerra repitió la lira con indómito cantar, guerra gritó al despertar el pueblo que al mundo aterra, y cuando en hispana tierra pasos extraños se oyeron, hasta las tumbas se abrieron gritando venganza y guerra . . .* All English translations in the text are mine.

(49) *Since the fatherland . . . avenge you*: The original Spanish lines are: *Pues que la patria lo quiere, lánzate al combate y muere, tu madre te vengará . . .*

(49–50) *Malaga . . . Cordoba*: Malaga, port city (and province) on the Costa del Sol of Andalusia in southern Spain. Seville, principal city (and province) of Andalusia on the Guadalquivir River, important historically as a capital and cultural center of Moorish Spain and a base for Spanish exploration of the New World. Cordoba, typical Moorish city (and province) of Andalusia, known for its mosque; a major commercial and cultural center in the Middle Ages.

(50) *Seneca . . . Manolete*: Lucius Annaeus Seneca (4 B.C.– A.D.65), Roman philosopher and statesman born in Cordoba, Spain, who expounded the philosophy of Stoicism. Manuel Rodríguez Sánchez, known as Manolete (1917–47), legendary Spanish bullfighter of the forties known for his courage and his austere artistry; he was killed in Linares at the age of thirty by the bull Islero.

(50) *Falangist*: Member of the Falangist party (Falange Española), the primary fascist movement of twentieth-century Spain, founded in 1933 by José Antonio Rivera; it evolved into the official state party of the Franco regime.

(50) *National Syndicalist doctrine*: Doctrine of the Falangist party, set forth in the manifesto of 1934, advocating the creation of a national syndicalist state, a strong government and military, and Spanish imperialist expansion, while rejecting the Republican constitution, party politics, Marxism, and capitalism.

(50) *José Antonio*: José Antonio Primo de Rivera (1903–36), son of the dictator Miguel Primo de Rivera and founder of the Spanish fascist party Falange Española. Executed by the Loyalists after the outbreak of the Civil War, his articles and speeches formed the doctrine of Franco's Nationalist movement in the years following the war.

(50) *Las Arenas . . . La Monumental*: The two most famous bullrings of Barcelona.

(51) *April Fair*: Traditional spring festival in Seville, known for its flamenco music and dance, bullfighting, parades, and other amusements.

(51) *flamenco*: An intense, rhythmic Andalusian dance created by the Gypsies of southern Spain.

(51) *Almería*: A Spanish province and port city on the eastern edge of Andalusia along the Mediterranean Sea.

(51) *sevillanas*: A four-part folk dance accompanied by guitar that is associated with Seville.

(51) *La Maestranza*: The famous bullring of Seville, one of the oldest in Spain (begun around 1760).

(52) *picador*: An assistant to the matador, who prods the bull with a lance to excite the animal in preparation for the kill.

(52) *Granada*: A major city and cultural center in Andalusia; the last great stronghold of the Moors in Spain, it fell to the Catholic Monarchs Ferdinand and Isabella in 1492.

(52) *you were sad and lonely . . . across the square*: The original Spanish verses of the narrator's poem are: *estabas triste y solo, eras callado y frío, yo te besé en los ojos y te robé una flor*; to which her teacher's poetic response was: *Nadie cruza la plaza ni turba su silencio. Todo es paz y sosiego y reposo y quietud. Sólo grácil y leve, en tus versos primeros, a través de la plaza, otra vez llegas tú.*

(52) *Alhambra . . . Albaicín*: Three important cultural sites of Granada. The Alhambra is a palace-citadel on a hill overlooking Granada, built by Ibn al-Ahmar of the Nasrid dynasty in the thirteenth century. The Generalife is the summer palace and gardens of the Alhambra. The Albaicín is the old Moorish quarter of Granada.

(52) *from Cádiz to Barcelona*: Cádiz is a major port city of Andalusia, located sixty miles northwest of Gibraltar on the Atlantic coast. Barcelona is the capital of Catalonia, Spain's second largest city and principal port, located on the northeastern Mediterranean coast; rich in history and culture, it is one of the leading intellectual and commercial centers of Spain.

(52) *Antonio Ordóñez* (1932–98): Famous Andalusian matador, considered to be the foremost bullfighter of the fifties and sixties. His father, also a well-known matador, knew Ernest Hemingway, who took a great interest in bullfighting.

(53) *the brothers Alvarez Quintero*: Serafín and Joaquín Alvarez Quintero (1871–1938, 1873–1944 respectively), born in Utrera (near Seville). Popular dramatists of the

Madrid theater, known for their colorful one-act plays and *zarzuelas* (Spanish musical dramas) highlighting Andalusian customs and way of life.

(54) *fandango*: A lively Spanish dance in triple time generally performed by a man and a woman with castanets.

(54–55) *Palillos . . . postizas*: Terms used by the Gypsies for castanets [*castañuelas*].

(55) *Bécquer*: Gustavo Adolfo Bécquer (1836–70), Spanish late Romantic poet and author from Seville, known for his *Rimas*, short intimist poems of great suggestiveness and depth of feeling on the themes of love and loneliness, the unfathomable mysteries of life and poetry.

(55) *Episodios Nacionales*: "National Episodes" (1873–1912), a series of forty-six historical novels by the Spanish realist author Benito Pérez Galdós (1843–1920), relating episodes in nineteenth-century Spanish history from the Battle of Trafalgar (1805) to the restoration of the Bourbon dynasty (1874).

(55) *Guzmán el Bueno*: Alonso Pérez de Guzmán (1256–1309), a brave warrior who played an important part in the reconquest of Spain from the Moors. In 1296 he defended the besieged town of Tarifa for King Sancho IV; when the Arabs threatened to kill one of his sons whom they held prisoner if he did not surrender, he allowed the youth to be murdered. He was rewarded by large land grants from the crown.

(55) *General Moscardó*: José Moscardó Ituarte (1878–1956), a Spanish general who allied himself with Franco in the Civil War. In 1936 he led the defense of the alcazar of Toledo, holding out for two months until the Nationalist forces arrived and liberated them.

(55) *Spartan child*: The story of a child who followed the Spartan code of bravery and fortitude. He captured a live fox and planned to eat it, but when he saw soldiers approaching he hid the fox underneath his shirt, and allowed the fox to chew into his stomach without showing any sign of pain rather than confess.

(56) *Saragossa . . . the Pilarica*: City in Aragon, northeastern Spain, on the Ebro River. One of the first towns in Spain to be Christianized, it had a church dedicated to the Virgin called "Nuestra Señora del Pilar" [Our Lady of the Pillar] in the first century A.D. and a bishop by the mid third century A.D. In the Peninsular War (1808–14) it was known for the heroic resistance of its citizens during a prolonged siege by the French (1808). There were some courageous female defenders of the city, such as Agustina de Aragón, known as the "Maid of Saragossa," who fired a cannon at the advancing French troops as her fiancé lay dying by her side; her exploits are related in Lord Byron's poem *Childe Harold's Pilgrimage* (1812–18). Tusquets' reference to the Pilarica alludes to a popular song from Aragon; the verse reads: *La Virgen del Pilar dice que no quiere ser francesa, que quiere ser capitana de la tropa aragonesa* [The Virgin of the Pillar says she does not want to be French; she wants to be captain of the Aragonese troops].

(56) *stolz wie ein Spanier*: German saying: proud as a Spaniard.

(56) *Carlos Barral* (1928–89): Spanish poet, prose writer, and director of Barral Editores (Barcelona), which became one of the most important European publishing houses of the latter half of the twentieth century.

(57) *paso doble*: A traditional Spanish dance with a man and a woman which mimics the movements of the Spanish bullfight, i.e., of the toreador and his cape.

(57) *Gothic quarter*: The old quarter of Barcelona, named for its great medieval buildings constructed between the thirteenth and the fifteenth centuries.

(58) *cloister of San Pablo*: The cloister of the main cathedral, a beautiful, light and airy interior garden with palm trees and magnolias, intricate wrought ironwork and huge bays.

(58) *Neither lilting river . . . gaze*: The original Spanish lines read: *Ni río cantarín, ni dulce ruiseñor, daban notas al aire embalsamado, sólo el silencio, eterno trovador, nos hechizaba con su canto alado . . . El claustro era escondido y solitario, las columnas muy finas y elevadas, las antiguas paredes del santuario conservan el ardor de sus/tus miradas.*

(59) *the three Marys*: A phrase used in the Franco period to denote three courses for university students required by the state for graduation: nationalist training, religion, and gymnastics.

(59) *There are more days than sausages*: An old Spanish adage: *Hay más días que longanizas.*

(60) *cortado*: Coffee with a dash of milk.

(61) *Montjuic*: A hill overlooking the port and city of Barcelona, topped with a seventeenth-century fortress castle.

(62) *Calderón*: Pedro Calderón de la Barca (1600–1681), the last great playwright of the Spanish Golden Age. A representative of the Counterreformation, his works combine Baroque disillusionment with the Christianizing trend of the period. His plays deal with moral and philosophical issues, such as the human struggle between reason (the mind or soul) and instinct (the body); in his view it is the triumph of the former over the latter which affords man "free will," thereby raising him above the animal world. His most famous plays are *La vida es sueño* [*Life is a Dream*] (1635), *El alcalde de Zalamea* [*The Mayor of Zalamea*] (c. 1640), and the auto sacramental *El gran teatro del mundo* [*The Great Theatre of the World*] (c. 1635).

(62) *¡Buen viaje!*: "Have a good trip!"

(62–63) *You have the name and body . . . Andalucía*: The original lines of the teacher's poem are: *Tienes nombre y cuerpo de mujer judía, cara nazarena de Virgen María. Eres, vida mía, cristiana y pagana como Andalucía.*

(63) *Julio Romero de Torres* (1874–1930): Spanish turn-of-the-century painter from Cordoba, known for his portraits of Andalusian women who represent for him an archetypal beauty.

(67) *Mis dos vidas by Berta Singerman*: "My Two Lives" (1981), the autobiography of Berta Singerman (1901–98), actress and rhapsodist born in Russia who emigrated as a child to Buenos Aires, Argentina. She became the most internationally acclaimed interpreter of Castilian poetry.

(68) *Sartre . . . Juliette Greco*: Jean-Paul Sartre (1905–80), French existentialist philosopher, novelist, and dramatist of the forties and fifties; his most famous works are the novel *La nausée* [*Nausea*] (1938), the philosophical treatise *L'être et le néant* [*Being and Nothingness*] (1943), and the plays *Les mouches* [*The Flies*] (1943) and *Huis clos* [*No Exit*] (1947). Albert Camus (1913–60), French Algerian existentialist novelist, essayist, and playwright of the forties and fifties, well known for his novels *L'Etranger* [*The Stranger*] (1942), *La Peste* [*The Plague*] (1947), and *La Chute* [*The Fall*] (1956), and for his work to promote leftist causes. Juliette Greco (1927–), legendary French *chanteuse* of literary and poetic texts, who led a Bohemian life in the Paris Latin Quarter among the foremost French artists and intellectuals of the postwar period.

(68) *La casa oscura*: "The Dark House."

(69) *Thumbelina . . . Snow White*: "Thumbelina" (1835), fairy tale by Hans Christian Andersen. "Hansel and Gretel" (first ed. 1812, final ed. 1857), fairy tale adapted by the German brothers Jacob and Wilhelm Grimm (1785–1863, 1786–1859 respectively). "Snow White" (first ed. 1812), fairy tale adapted by the Brothers Grimm. In early editions of "Hansel and Gretel" and "Snow White" the evil parental figure was the mother, while in later editions it was changed to the stepmother, apparently to tone down the story for children.

(69) *Hippolytus*: Hero of the ancient Greek tragedy *Hippolytus* (428 B.C.) by Euripides (c. 485–406 B.C.). Because Hippolytus spurns Aphrodite, the goddess of love, she punishes him by having his stepmother Phaedra fall in love with him. When the young man reacts with horror to this news Phaedra kills herself, leaving behind a note accusing him of dishonoring her, which leads to his being condemned to exile and death by his bereft father King Theseus.

(69) *the chaste Joseph*: Son of the Hebrews Jacob and Rachel in the Old Testament book of Genesis. Sold into slavery by his brothers, he gains a favorable position in the household of Potiphar, an officer of the Egyptian Pharoah. However when he rejects the advances of his master's wife, she accuses him of attempting to dishonor her, and her incensed husband puts him in prison. Later he is freed and elevated in rank by the Pharoah himself.

(71) *Pamplona . . . Tarragona*: Pamplona is the capital of Navarre, located in the Pyrenees Mountains of northeastern Spain. San Sebastián is an elegant resort city on the Bay of Biscay in the Basque country, very near the border with France. Madrid is the capital city of Spain, located on the central plateau of the Iberian Peninsula. Tarragona is a port city in Catalonia; it was the earliest Roman stronghold in Spain.

(72) *Lorca*: Federico García Lorca (1898–1936), native of Granada, the greatest dramatist and poet of twentieth-century Spain. Most of his works (such as his book of poetry *Romancero gitano* [*Gypsy Ballads*] (1928)) are deeply Andalusian in atmosphere, evoking a primitive semi-mythical world moved by mysterious dark forces. His poetry

and dramas combine elements of folklore with innovative and often surrealistic poetic techniques. A pervasive theme is the tense kinship of love and death. In his three rural tragedies: *Bodas de sangre* [*Blood Wedding*] (1935), *Yerma* (1937), and *La casa de Bernarda Alba* [*The House of Bernarda Alba*] (1940), he shows how the inner conflict caused by society's repression of the vital instincts and passions inevitably culminates in destruction and violent death. He was executed as an intellectual by Franco's Nationalists at the start of the Civil War.

(72) *la Xirgu*: Margarita Xirgu (1888–1969), brilliant Spanish actress from Catalonia. She worked in Barcelona, then in the Madrid theater, acting in and directing the classics as well as contemporary works, and soon gained renown throughout Spain and the Americas. Upon the outbreak of the Spanish Civil War she went into voluntary exile; she spent the rest of her life working in Argentina and Uruguay. A friend of García Lorca, she performed the female lead in his rural tragedies and sought to promote his work; after his death she staged the world premiere of *The House of Bernarda Alba* in Buenos Aires (1945).

(74) *Cochabamba*: A largely agricultural city located in a fertile basin of the Andes Mountains of central Bolivia.

(76) *"La marcha triunfal"*: "Triumphal March," a poem from *Cantos de vida y esperanza* (1905) by the Nicaraguan poet Rubén Darío (1867–1916), the most influential modernist poet writing in Spanish.

(77) *All My Sons . . . Arthur Miller*: A 1947 drama by the American playwright Arthur Miller (1915–2005) which shows the moral dilemma of a man who during the Second World War knowingly authorized the use of defective parts from his factory in warplanes, leading to the death of many pilots, rather than risk his family's prosperity..

(77) *Sastre . . . Buero*: Alfonso Sastre (1926–) and Antonio Buero Vallejo (1916–2000), major Spanish postwar playwrights. Sastre wrote subversive plays of social and political criticism. Buero Vallejo, considered the most important Spanish dramatist of his generation, wrote socially committed and existentialist plays on contemporary and historical subjects.

(77) *costumbrismo*: A literary genre that features the local customs of various regions of Spain.

(77) *La herida luminosa . . . En Flandes se ha puesto el sol*: "The Shining Wound," 1956 drama by Josep María de Sagarra (1894–1961), a Catalan playwright, poet, and novelist from Barcelona. *A Saint in a Hurry*, 1933 drama in verse about the life of the Spanish Jesuit priest Saint Francis Xavier of Assisi by José María Pemán [see (45], a vehicle for the author's conservative beliefs regarding Catholic imperial Spain. "The Sun Has Set in Flanders," 1911 play by the Barcelonese poet-dramatist Eduardo Marquina (1879–1946), known for his dramatization of historical legends.

(78) *Alberti . . . Casona*: Rafael Alberti (1902–99), Spanish poet of the Generation of 1927, who spent much of his life in exile in Argentina and Italy. His most highly regarded works are difficult abstract and sometimes surrealist poetry; also a painter, some of his poetry was inspired by painting. Alejandro Casona, pseudonym of Alejan-

dro Rodríguez Alvarez (1900–65), Spanish playwright from Asturias known for the lyricism of his dramas and the interplay of reality, fantasy, and dream; he too went into exile in Buenos Aires following the Spanish Civil War.

(78) *Teatro Romea*: Theater in downtown Barcelona which has been a center for Catalan language drama since its founding in 1864.

(79) *Gray Wolf . . . Kazan*: Characters from *Kazan the Wolf Dog* (1914) by James Oliver Curwood (1878–1927), an American novelist who wrote popular books about northwestern Canada.

(80) *Neverland*: Home of Peter Pan, mythical child hero of the 1904 fairy play *Peter Pan* by the Scottish writer Sir James Barrie (1860–1937).

(80) *Marsillach*: Adolfo Marsillach Soriano (1928–2002), distinguished theater and movie director and actor from Barcelona who directed the Teatro Español, the Centro Dramático Nacional, and the Compañía Nacional de Teatro Clásico; he is renowned for his staging of world classics.

(80) *Ramblas*: The famous promenade in Barcelona, which winds its way down from the Plaça de Catalunya to the harbor and statue of Columbus. The colorful tree-lined street is full of cafés, kiosks, flower and animal stalls, and all kinds of street entertainers; it is a favorite gathering place for locals and tourists alike.

(81) *Palau*: Palau de la Música Catalana, splendid modernist concert hall in Barcelona, designed from 1905 to 1908 by the architect Luis Doménech y Montaner. Oscar Tusquets did a beautiful remodeling of the building in the eighties.

(84) *Proust . . . The Fruits of the Earth*: Marcel Proust (1871–1922), author of the vast modernist narrative cycle *A la recherche du temps perdu* [*Remembrance of Things Past*] (1913–27); generally regarded as the greatest French author of the twentieth century. Jean Genet (1910–86), French avant-garde playwright, novelist, and poet, considered a writer of the French "theater of the absurd." *Les nourritures terrestres* (1897), a lyrical didactic work exalting beauty and the life of the senses by the French novelist André Gide (1869–1951). Lorca and these French authors were all homosexuals.

(85) *Paseo de Gracia*: Fashionable promenade of Barcelona, constructed in the early to mid nineteenth century.

(87) *Barbary Pirate . . . Flying Dutchman*: Barbarossa [Red Beard], nickname of the Berber Khair ad Din (d. 1546), the most famous of the pirates who preyed on shipping in the western Mediterranean Sea from the Crusades until the early nineteenth century, their stronghold being the piece of north Africa known as the Barbary Coast. Sandokan, hero of Emilio Salgari's novel *Sandokan, The Tiger of Malaysia* (1883–84), a Malayan pirate. The Flying Dutchman was a legendary sea captain doomed to sail the seven seas forever; the legend became the subject of Wagner's 1843 opera *The Flying Dutchman*.

(87) *Bayreuth company*: Theater company from Bayreuth, Germany, where Richard Wagner built his festival theater in the 1870s to house productions of his operatic works.

(87) *Teatro Liceo*: The grand opera hall of Barcelona, built in the 1840s in the center of the Rambla by the architect Miguel Garriga i Roca; symbol of the Catalan upper-middle class. Destroyed by fire in 1994, it has now been fully restored.

(88) *distress . . . Siegfried*: In Wagner's *Ring* cycle, Siegfried and Brünnhilde fall in love and pledge their troth; it is through the subsequent intervention of a love potion administered by Siegfried's enemies that the hero forgets Brünnhilde and agrees to win her for Gunther in exchange for the hand of Gunther's sister Gutrune.

(89) *Sección Femenina*: The women's branch of the Falangist party, which was de-signed to train Spanish women for their proper role as wives and mothers through mandatory courses and social work.

(90) *Day of the Epiphany*: January 6, the last day of the Christmas season, which cel-ebrates the visit of the Three Magi to the infant Jesus in Bethlehem.

(91) *Sanfander*: A port city in Cantabria on the Bay of Biscay, on the northern coast of Spain.

(91) *Diálogos en la penumbra*: "Dialogues in the Shadows." Tusquets uses the title of this unpublished work as the subtitle of her "Letter to Eduardo."

(91) *Beauvoir*: Simone de Beauvoir (1908–86), French writer and philosopher, life-long companion of the existentialist Sartre, and the mother of French feminism with her groundbreaking treatise *The Second Sex* [*Le deuxième sexe*] (1949).

(93) *an angel's plumes*: There is word play in the original Spanish phrase *plumas de ángel*, because the Spanish word *pluma* means both "feather" and "pen."

(94) *Ithaca*: The ancient Greek kingdom of Odysseus [Ulysses] in Homer's epic poem *The Odyssey* (first transcribed c. 800 B.C.).

(94) *gauche divine*: A group of Spanish left-wing intellectuals and artists who con-gregated in the cafés of Barcelona in the sixties and seventies.

(95) *La Mariona . . . Jamboree*: Famous Barcelona restaurant and nightclub.

(95) *Troy . . . Menelaus*: Troy is an ancient city in northwestern Anatolia, site of the legendary Trojan War which forms the basis of the Homeric epic poem *The Iliad* (first transcribed c. 800 B.C.). According to Greek legend, Paris was the son of King Priam of Troy and his wife Hecuba; his elopement with Helen (wife of King Menelaus of Sparta, considered to be the most beautiful woman of ancient Greece), in fulfillment of a promise made by the goddess Aphrodite, was the cause of the Trojan War.

(95) *Maresme . . . Vallès*: The Maresme is a Mediterranean coastal region just north-east of Barcelona, known for its agriculture and its scenic hills, beaches, and seashore. The Vallès is the region just inland from the mountains of the city. The Barcelonese bourgeoisie often had second homes in these two areas near the city.

(96) *Penelope . . . Ulysses*: In Greek mythology, Penelope was the faithful wife of Ulysses, ruler of Ithaca. During his long absence after the Trojan War, she avoided taking a new husband by insisting on first completing a mourning shroud for Laertes,

the father of Ulysses; she wove the shroud by day and unraveled what she had done by night. Ulysses is the hero of *The Odyssey*: a man of wisdom, astuteness, ingenuity, and courage, he wanders for many years and survives many adventures before finally returning home to reclaim his wife and son Telemachus and the kingdom of Ithaca.

(96) *Inés . . . Brígida*: Characters from the nineteenth-century drama *Don Juan Tenorio* (1844) by José Zorrilla (1817–93), popular Spanish Romantic poet and dramatist from Valladolid. In Zorrilla's version of the story Don Juan is redeemed through the pure love of the novice Doña Inés. Brígida is the duenna of Inés.

(96) *Senta*: The heroine of Wagner's opera *The Flying Dutchman* [see (87]. She saves the Dutchman from the curse of sailing the seven seas forever by offering him a love faithful unto death.

(97) *the prison of Montjuic*: A seventeenth-century fortress (expanded in the eighteenth century) used as a political prison until the time of General Franco; known for its horrors of starvation, torture and summary executions.

(98) *April 14, 1931*: On this date Spain was declared a republic following the deposition of King Alfonso XIII.

(98) *Che Guevara*: Ernesto "Che" Guevara (1928–67), revolutionary leader and guerilla fighter from Argentina. He took part in the Cuban Revolution (1958–59) to overthrow the dictatorship of Fulgencio Batista, as well as other Latin American revolutionary causes.

(99) *Aminta . . . Dido*: Aminta is a village maiden betrothed to Batricio in Tirso de Molina's play *El burlador de Sevilla* [*The Playboy of Seville*] (c. 1630); Don Juan steals into her bed before the wedding day. Tisbea is a fisherman's daughter in the same play who saves Don Juan after he is shipwrecked on the Spanish coast; he seduces her by promising her marriage and then escapes. Inés: see (96. In Greek mythology Calypso was a sea nymph and queen of the island of Ogygia. Lover of the shipwrecked Ulysses, she tried to keep him forever by promising him immortality, but he refused, longing for his homeland and his wife Penelope; she detained him for seven years, until Zeus ordered her to let him go and she reluctantly obeyed. Circe was a Greek sorceress who had the power to transform men into beasts; Ulysses escaped her evil charms but was seduced by her and lived with her for a year before resuming his journey homeward. Nausicaa, daughter of the rulers of Phaeacia, finding Ulysses shipwrecked by the shore of a river took him back to the palace of her father, King Alcinous, who gave him a ship for his return to Ithaca. Enamored of the hero, the virtuous young princess regretfully accepted his departure, knowing he could not be hers since he was married to another. In Virgil's *Aeneid* (c. 19 B.C.), Dido was the queen of Carthage who fell in love with Aeneas when he landed on her shore. When he departed without taking leave of her upon the order of Zeus, she stabbed herself upon a flaming funeral pyre.

(101) *Costa Brava*: The northernmost part of the Mediterranean coast of Spain extending almost to the French border; known for its beaches and its scenic and rugged coastline.

(102) *Mary Poppins*: The protagonist of the children's book series *Mary Poppins* (1934–88) by the Australian author Pamela L. Travers (1899–1996), about a magical British nanny who takes care of four children living in London.

(102) *the mystery of Elche*: A Spanish religious musical drama depicting the death, assumption and crowning of the Virgin Mary, performed since the fifteenth century in the Basilica of Saint Mary of Elche in Valencia.

(102) *walking on water . . . the dead bury their dead*: Events and sayings from the life of Jesus of Nazareth as recorded in the New Testament.

(102) *the Song of Songs*: The Old Testament Song of Solomon.

(104) *Daughter of Mary*: A religious association active during the Franco period for Catholic girls aspiring to a life of piety and good deeds inspired by the Virgin Mary. Girls generally entered the organization at about the age of sixteen and remained members until their marriage.

(105) *Rota tribunal of Rome or Madrid*: The supreme ecclesiastical court of the Roman Catholic Church for cases appealed to the Holy See from diocesan courts. Since 1774 there has been a Rota tribunal in Madrid, the president of which is the Nuncio.

(110) *Fate l'amore, no l'editore*: "Make love; don't publish." The publisher is Feltrinelli, an important Milan publishing house of the second half of the twentieth century that pursued literary innovation and cutting-edge politics.

(110) *Perpignan*: City in southern France, at the northeastern edge of the Pyrenees Mountains twelve kilometers west of the Mediterranean and near the border with Spain. It served as a cultural haven for Spanish artists and intellectuals during the repressive Franco regime.

(110) *Ruedo Ibérico*: A radical Spanish publishing house that spent many years of the Franco regime in exile in Paris. They put out a left-wing magazine called *Cuadernos de Ruedo Ibérico* to which many important writers of the period contributed.

(110) *To Die in Madrid . . . Crazy Horse*: *To Die in Madrid* [*Mourir à Madrid*] is a vivid 1963 documentary on the Spanish Civil War by the French director Frédéric Rossif. *Night and Fog* [*Nuit et brouillard*] is Alain Resnais' powerful 1955 documentary on the horrors of the World War II Nazi concentration camps. *The Battleship Potemkin* (1925) is Sergei Eisenstein's groundbreaking film on the Potemkin mutiny, part of the failed 1905 uprising in Czarist Russia; the film was intended as part of a cycle telling the story of the Russian Revolution. Jeanne Moreau (1928–) plays the heroine of Louis Malle's 1958 French film *The Lovers* [*Les amants*] about a woman's discovery of romantic love in an adulterous affair. Crazy Horse is an elegant Parisian cabaret known for its all-female dance revue.

(110) *Living Theater . . . copulation*: An experimental off-Broadway repertory group established in New York in 1951 by Julian Beck (1925–85) and his wife Judith Malina (1926–); in the sixties they left the United States and became very influential in European theater. These lines are from their 1968 production *Paradise Now*, which aimed to promote a peaceful anarchist revolution by freeing the individual.

(110) *Bocaccio*: Renowned Barcelona nightclub.

(110) *the opinionated female poet . . . Vallès*: The Catalan poet is Marta Pessarrodona (1941–) from Terrassa (Vallès), who was also a Woolf expert and a translator. Virginia Woolf (1882–1941) was a British modernist writer who experimented with form and style to express the flow of inner and outer experience. She and her husband Leonard formed the literary circle called the Bloomsbury group at her family home in Gordon Square, London. The Spanish *gauche divine* of the sixties and seventies was based in Barcelona and some towns of the Vallès.

(110) *Fellinesque parties*: A reference to the wild and orgiastic parties in the films of the Italian director Federico Fellini (1920–93), which reveal the superficiality and decadence of modern Rome.

(111) *clay whistle dolls*: Majorcan human or animal figures made of clay with a whistle (known as "Siurells"), which were very popular in the sixties.

(113) *the water nymph . . . Giraudoux*: From the play *Ondine* (1939) by the French dramatist and novelist Jean Giraudoux (1882–1944), based on La Motte-Fouqué's fairy tale about a water nymph who loves a mortal man.

(114) *Wilde*: Oscar Wilde (1854–1900), Irish wit, playwright and poet who was an exponent of late nineteenth-century Aestheticism in England, the belief in art for art's sake. He is known for his society comedies *Lady Windermere's Fan* (1892) and *The Importance of Being Earnest* (1895), his novel *The Picture of Dorian Gray* (1891), and his collection of allegorical fairy tales *The Happy Prince and Other Tales* (1888).

(114) *Princess Aurora*: The name given to Sleeping Beauty in the 1910 version of the fairy tale by Sir Arthur Quiller-Couch (1863–1944); Aurora means "the dawn."

(115) *Tetrarchs . . . Florian*: Renowned landmarks of Venice, Italy. The Tetrarchs are sculptures of porphyry (Egypt, fourth century A.D.) of four emperors (Diocletian, Maximilian, Constantius, and Valerius) who ruled the Roman Empire jointly in the late third century A.D.; located in a corner of the façade of Saint Mark's Basilica, they are seen embracing in a gesture of equality and harmony. Saint Mark's is a magnificent Byzantine church in the heart of Venice with five domes and splendid exterior and interior decoration, begun in the eleventh century on the site of the original ninth-century church, which was destroyed by fire. The Doge's Palace was the residence of the head of the Venetian city-state and the seat of government; the original ninth-century palace was destroyed by fire and was completely rebuilt in the fourteenth and fifteenth centuries. The Bellini is a drink consisting of white peach juice and sparkling wine, a specialty of Harry's Bar, a famous bar on the waterfront of St. Mark's Square. The Florian is an historical café situated beneath the porticoes of St. Mark's Square.

(118) *Victor Hugo . . . aimer*: Prolific French poet, novelist, and playwright (1802–85), that country's most important and influential Romantic author. "I have nothing more to do here on earth but to love."

(118) *Brassens*: Georges Brassens (1921–81), revered French singer and songwriter, known for his fine songs and articulate lyrics; regarded as one of the best postwar poets of France.

(118) *Piaf . . . Olympia*: Edith Piaf, byname of Edith Giovanna Gassion (1915–63), beloved singer of French sentimental ballads or *chansons*. She captivated audiences with the raw passion of her voice and presence in songs which gave musical expression to her own life experience. The Olympia is the oldest Parisian music hall, the place where Piaf gained fame and where she gave some of her most moving concerts in the period before her death from cancer.

(118) *Assyrian reliefs at the British Museum*: Polychrome carved stone reliefs used to decorate imperial monuments in ancient Mesopotamia, depicting royal affairs like hunting and waging war; some of the best known examples (from the ninth and seventh centuries B.C.) are in the British Museum in London.

(118) *felucca*: A narrow, swift lateen-rigged sailing ship typically used in the Mediterranean Sea.

(118) *Cap de Creus*: A rugged cape at the foot of the Pyrenees on the Mediterranean Sea very near the border with France.

(118) *Visconti*: Luchino Visconti (1906–76), Italian film director regarded as the father of postwar Neorealism, and innovative stage and opera director.

(118) *Bergman . . . Wild Strawberries*: Ingmar Bergman (1918–), Swedish movie writer-director and theater director known for his compelling camera work and deep exploration of the human psyche, his highly personal vision of loneliness and spiritual angst, the quest for communion and meaning. *Wild Strawberries* (1957) is his meditation on aging, time, life and death, as seen in an old man's inner journey through past and present, memory and dream.

(118) *Béjart . . . Rites of Spring*: Maurice Béjart, pseudonym of Maurice-Jean de Berger (1928–), French dancer, choreographer, and opera director known for his innovative blend of classic ballet with modern dance, jazz, and acrobatics. After his acclaimed 1959 ballet production of Igor Stravinsky's *Rites of Spring* he became director of ballet at Brussels' Théâtre Royal de la Monnaie and artistic director of the Ballet of the Twentieth Century, which became one of the greatest dance companies in the world.

(118) *Faust of Strehler*: Giorgio Strehler (1921–2002), Italian theater director who founded the Piccolo Theater in 1947 with Paolo Grassi, where he developed his idea of a theater of high aesthetic quality that would appeal to people of all social classes. He staged many world classics, including Goethe's *Faust*, parts one and two, in which he played the leading role.

(118) *Antigone of the Living Theater*: A 1967 adaptation of Bertolt Brecht's (1948) adaptation of the original Sophocles play by Judith Malina, cofounder of the experimental Living Theater in New York [see (110)]. Written while she was in jail for political protest, the action was designed to evoke comparisons with the contemporaneous Vietnam War.

(118) *sculptures of the Medici Chapels*: Sculptures by Michelangelo Buonarroti (1475–1564) that adorn the tombs of some members of the Medici family in the New Sacristy

of the Church of San Lorenzo in Florence, Italy; the most exquisite are the allegories of Day, Night, Dawn, and Dusk.

(118) *Parthenon*: Ancient Greek temple on the hill of the Acropolis, built to honor Athena Parthenos, the patron goddess of Athens. Erected under Pericles between 447 B.C. and 432 B.C., it is regarded as the supreme example of Doric architecture.

(120) *Marsé*: Juan Marsé (1933–), realist novelist from Barcelona who depicts the material and moral bankruptcy of postwar Spain under the Franco regime.

(120) *Marítim*: Name of a popular bar by the sea in the center of Cadaqués, a scenic town at the foot of the Pyrenees on the Costa Brava near the French border.

(120) *Tour de France*: Famous French bicycle race established in 1903 by Henri Desgranges (1865–1940), covering about 2,500 miles of flat and mountainous countryside in France and surrounding countries.

Select Bibliography

First Editions of
Tusquets' Literary Works

El mismo mar de todos los veranos. Barcelona: Editorial Lumen, 1978.

El amor es un juego solitario. Barcelona: Lumen, 1979.

Varada tras el último naufragio. Barcelona: Lumen, 1980.

La conejita Marcela. Barcelona: Lumen, 1980.

Siete miradas en un mismo paisaje. Barcelona: Lumen, 1981.

Para no volver. Barcelona: Lumen, 1985.

La reina de los gatos. Barcelona: Lumen, 1993.

"Carta a la madre." In *Madres e hijas*, edited by Laura Freixas, 75–93. Barcelona: Editorial Anagrama, 1996.

"La niña lunática" y otros cuentos. Barcelona: Lumen, 1997.

Con la miel en los labios. Barcelona: Anagrama, 1997.

Correspondencia privada. Barcelona: Anagrama, 2001.

"Orquesta de verano" y otros cuentos. Barcelona: Plaza y Janés Editores, 2002.

Confesiones de una editora poco mentirosa. Barcelona: RqueR Editorial, 2005.

English Translations of
Tusquets' Novels and Stories

The Same Sea as Every Summer. Translated by Margaret E. W. Jones. Lincoln: University of Nebraska Press, 1990.

Love Is a Solitary Game. Translated by Bruce Penman. New York: Riverrun Press, 1985.

Stranded. Translated by Susan E. Clark. Elmwood Park, IL: Dalkey Archive Press, 1991.

"Summer orchestra." Translated by Margaret Jull Costa. In *The Origins of Desire: Modern Spanish Short Stories*, edited by Juan Antonio Masoliver, 80–90. London: Serpent's Tail, 1993.

Never to Return. Translated by Barbara F. Ichiishi. Lincoln: University of Nebraska Press, 1999.

INTERVIEWS WITH TUSQUETS

Verdu, Vicente. "'Los adultos no sabemos amar.'" *Cuadernos para el diálogo*, June 10, 1978, 52–53.

Moix, Ana María. "Esther Tusquets: Madame Lumen para los amigos." *El viejo topo* 24 (September 1978): 64–67.

Elu, Arantza. "Esther Tusquets, amor y literatura para poder vivir." *Ere* 36 May 21–28, 1980).

Sala, Montserrat. "'La soledad es la ausencia del amor y el predominio de la muerte.'" *El noticiero universal*, August 24, 1981.

Dolgin, Stacey L. "Conversación con Esther Tusquets: 'Para salir de tanta miseria.'" *Anales de la literatura española contemporanea* 13, no. 3 (1988): 397–406.

Rodríguez, Mercedes Mazquiarán de. "Entrevista con Esther Tusquets." *Letras Peninsulares* 13, no. 2 (Fall 2000): 609–19.

SECONDARY SOURCES

Bellver, Catherine G. "The Language of Eroticism in the Novels of Esther Tusquets." *Anales de la literatura española contemporanea* 9, nos. 1–3 (1984): 13–27.

———. "Assimilation and Confrontation in Esther Tusquets's *Para no volver*." *Romanic Review* 81, no. 3 (May 1990): 368–76.

Casado, Stacey Dolgin. *Squaring the Circle: Esther Tusquets' Novelistic Tetralogy (A Jungian Analysis)*. Newark, DE: Juan de la Cuesta, 2002.

García Jambrina, Luis. "Cuatro cartas abiertas." *ABC Cultural*, June 2, 2001, 11.

Hart, Stephen M. "Spain." In *The Bloomsbury Guide to Women's Literature*, edited by Clare Buck, 76–80. New York: Prentice Hall, 1992.

Ichiishi, Barbara F. *The Apple of Earthly Love: Female Development in Esther Tusquets' Fiction*. New York: Peter Lang, 1994.

Lee-Bonanno, Lucy. "The Renewal of the Quest in Esther Tusquets' *El mismo mar de todos los veranos*." In *Feminine Concerns in Contemporary Spanish Fiction by Women*, edited by Robert C. Manteiga, Carolyn Galerstein, and Kathleen McNerney, 134–51. Potomac, MD: Scripta Humanística,1988.

Miller, Nancy. *But Enough About Me: Why We Read Other People's Lives*. New York: Columbia University Press, 2002.

Moix, Ana María. *Julia*. Barcelona: Seix Barral, 1969.

———. "El mar común de todas las historias." *El País* May 19, 2001, 5.

Molinaro, Nina L. *Foucault, Feminism, and Power: Reading Esther Tusquets*. Lewisburg, PA: Bucknell University Press, 1991.

Navajas, Gonzalo. "Repetition and the Rhetoric of Love in Esther Tusquets' *El mismo mar de todos los veranos*." In *Nuevos y novísimos: Algunas perspectivas críticas sobre la narrativa española desde la década de los 60*, edited by Ricardo Landeira and Luis T. González-del-Valle, 113–29. Boulder, CO: Society of Spanish and Spanish-American Studies, 1987.

Ordóñez, Elizabeth J. "A Quest for Matrilineal Roots and Mythopoesis: Esther Tusquets' *El mismo mar de todos los veranos*." *Crítica Hispánica* 6, no. 1 (Spring 1984):
37–46.

Servodidio, Mirella d'Ambrosio. "Perverse Pairings and Corrupted Codes: *El amor es
un juego solitario*." *Anales de la literatura española contemporanea* 11, no. 3 (1986):
237–54.

———. "A Case of Pre-oedipal and Narrative Fixation: *El mismo mar de todos los veranos*." *Anales de la literatura española contemporanea* 12, nos. 1–2 (1987): 157–74.

———. "Esther Tusquets' Fiction: The Spinning of a Narrative Web." In *Women
Writers of Contemporary Spain: Exiles in the Homeland*, edited by Joan L. Brown,
159–78. Newark: University of Delaware Press, 1991.

———. "Esther Tusquets, *Correspondencia privada*." *Revista Hispánica Moderna* 60, no.
1 (June 2002): 223–24.

Tsuchiya, Akiko. "Theorizing the Feminine: Esther Tusquets's *El mismo mar de todos los
veranos* and Hélène Cixous's *écriture féminine*." *Revista de estudios hispánicos* 26, no. 2
(May 1992): 183–99.

Vásquez, Mary S., ed. *The Sea of Becoming: Approaches to the Fiction of Esther Tusquets*.
Westport, CT: Greenwood Press, 1991.

Vosburg, Nancy B. "*Siete miradas en un mismo paisaje* de Esther Tusquets: Hacia un
proceso de individuación." *Monographic Review* 4 (1988): 97–106.